P9-DEN-313

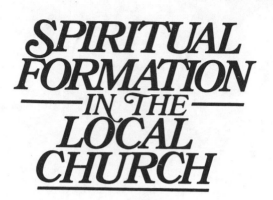

SPIRITUAL FORMATION IN THE LOCAL CHURCH

SPIRITUAL FORMATION IN THE LOCAL CHURCH

Frank Bateman Stanger

FRANCIS ASBURY PRESS
of Zondervan Publishing House
Grand Rapids, Michigan

Spiritual Formation in the Local Church
Copyright © 1989 by Mardelle A. Stanger

Francis Asbury Press is an imprint of Zondervan Publishing House,
1415 Lake Drive, S.E., Grand Rapids, Michigan 49506.

Library of Congress Cataloging in Publication Data

Stanger, Frank Bateman.
  Spiritual formation in the local church / Frank Bateman Stanger.
    p.   cm.
  ISBN 0-310-75451-8
  1. Spiritual formation—Methodist Church. I. Title.
BV4511.S72   1989
253.5'3–dc20   89-11865
                                                                      CIP

All rights reserved. No part of this publication may be reproduced, stored in a
retrieval system, or transmitted in any form or by any means—electronic,
mechanical, photocopy, recording, or any other—except for brief quotations in
printed reviews, without the prior permission of the publisher.

Edited by Joe Comanda

Printed in the United States of America

89 90 91 92 93 94 95 / CH / 10 9 8 7 6 5 4 3 2 1

CONTENTS

Bookstore

81997

Frank Bateman Stanger died before he was able to finish the citations. His former secretary, Mrs. Harriett Jenkins, of Lexington, Kentucky, and Mrs. Eunice Weldon, research librarian at the B. L. Fisher Library at Asbury Theological Seminary, have been of immeasurable assistance. However, some notes are incomplete and a number of quotations have been impossible to trace.

INTRODUCTION

Both author and reader need to have a clear understanding of why a book is written. This is especially true for the serious reader in the spiritual realm. Such a reader does not wish to waste time reading pointless books, however novel their content.

This is a book about spiritual growth, and it has a definite purpose. Unlike most books on the subject, it is not primarily about *personal* spiritual growth, though its pages have much to offer a reader on that subject. Rather, it is about spiritual growth in the church as a whole. Thus, instead of providing a series of spiritual techniques for personal growth, it seeks to foster an awareness of the need for *church-wide* spiritual growth and a *church-wide* plan for spiritual formation.

I am writing out of a twofold personal experience: a lifelong concern for personal spiritual growth and a recent experiment in developing a church-wide plan of spiritual growth.

I have been a Christian for more than six decades and a minister of the gospel for more than a half-century. My entire life and ministry have had a basic focus upon spirituality.

I was reared in a godly home where we observed family worship daily. We attended faithfully all the services of the local Methodist church—four on Sunday, two during the week, and a protracted revival meeting annually. In addition, Christian literature came to our home regularly, and it was a part of our spiritual diet.

In the summertime I attended camp meetings. Of course, the primary emphasis there was on "hitting the trail" (getting into a right relationship with the Lord). Sinners needed to be converted, backsliders needed to be reclaimed, believers needed to be sanctified wholly. But once the needed spiritual experience was entered into, we were exhorted to "grow in the grace and knowledge of our Lord Jesus Christ."

During all of these early years of my spiritual pilgrimage, I was developing personal devotional habits. I learned it was better to pray in the morning than to fall asleep on my knees at bedtime. I remember the relief of being convinced that it was all right to underline my Bible as I read it devotionally. I began collecting and reading pamphlets and books containing devotional gems. I recall several occasions when I read such writings while pushing a lawn mower (no power mower in those days). I emulated the example of the early circuit riders who read as they rode by reading as I walked. (And actually the mowed paths across the lawn were amazingly straight and even.)

I attended a Christian college that placed a strong emphasis on personal spirituality. We had two revival series each school year, class prayer meetings twice a week, and a college prayer meeting once a week. Each college class began with prayer. Dorm bulletin boards displayed devotional writings. The college book-store featured books in the area of spirituality. In those formative years I began my now-extensive collection of devotional writings.

I was an active Methodist pastor serving local churches for nearly a quarter of a century. I believe that officials and members from all of the churches I served would bear witness to my ministerial focus upon spiritual experience and the Christian's life. This emphasis could also be clearly established by a study of the topics in my sermon index and certainly by an examination of the content of my preaching.

I have always been a preacher in the Wesleyan tradition. Early in my ministry I became convinced that an emphasis upon spirituality was at the heart of the Methodist movement, and my continuing Wesleyan studies through the years have both confirmed and deepened this conviction.

In passing, let me pay tribute to the leadership of one of our contemporary Methodist pioneers in the revival of concern for spirituality in our churches. On numerous occasions, the Rev. Dr. G. Ernest Thomas invited me to participate with him in Spiritual Life Conferences. Those experiences never failed to stimulate my desire for effective spiritual leadership wherever I was privileged to serve.

During the second half of my active ministry I had the high privilege of serving as president and professor at one of America's influential theological seminaries. It is a seminary with a tradition—a tradition born in the fires of the Methodist Revival, a tradition cherished and held onto during more recent years of liberal theology and pluralistic religious lifestyles, a tradition which remains God's beacon light for growth and effective ministry in the training of tomorrow's preachers.

I never would have felt at home in my administration of this theological school had I not been heartily congenial to every legitimate Wesleyan influence, but I threw the full weight of my leadership on the side of developing spirituality among the seminary family.

Near the end of my administration at the seminary I came to a new realization. Fostering personal spiritual growth within each seminarian was not enough. The entire community needed to participate in structured spiritual development. To that end, we formed a Spiritual Life Committee, which I chaired, and we inaugurated a campus-wide program of spiritual formation, which is still active today.

At the close of the first year of the program, the student newspaper, *The Short Circuit,* carried an editorial in its April-May 1981 issue entitled, "The Asbury Revival of 1980–81." The editor commented:

> There were no TV cameras or radio newspeople, no newspaper reporters busy questioning students about their religious experience . . . In fact it almost got by me and I live in its presence. . . .
>
> Maybe you haven't noticed the revival. Well, just in case that is true let me give you a hint as to where to look. Look in spiritual formation groups. Some of them started last year even before the concept was talked about. Listen as people talk about how for the first time in their lives they are having a consistent quiet time. Watch their eyes as they tell you how for the first time in their lives they can tell people they have sinned, or they hurt, or they need. Feel love and wholeness as it flashes from their eyes to yours, and as they reach out no longer afraid to touch and be touched. Smell the sweet fragrance in the air as you move through your day. It is a fragrance of love you know. People in love with themselves, and others, and you. There is a revival at Asbury Seminary.

As the time approached for my retirement from both the seminary presidency and my annual conference, I thought prayerfully about possible priorities in my post-retirement ministries. I became increasingly convinced that a basic need in the life and work of the local church was in the area of spiritual formation. I became enamored of the idea of establishing an institute of spirituality for the training of both clergy and laity. I even solicited funds, but to no avail.

But the dream remained alive within my mind and heart into my retirement days. When I was approached about assuming a staff position at Centenary United Methodist Church in Lexington, Kentucky, a church with 2,500 members, I accepted with the understanding that I could inaugurate a church-wide plan of spiritual formation. I served as Minister of Spiritual Formation at Centenary Church from February 1983 until May 1984.

In this book I want to share what I call the Centenary Model. After discussing the spiritual considerations that motivated my leadership in spiritual formation in the first place, I want to tell the story step-by-step of how the Centenary Model was formulated and implemented. I will also include samples of materials we used in the program. Then in the concluding section I want to share with you the lessons we learned from our experience with the Centenary Model. I will deal candidly with both the principles and pitfalls we discovered.

It is my sincere hope that this book will be both a stimulus to the Christian's concern for spiritual formation and a guide book for the local church to help it provide its members with structured and continuing opportunities for such spiritual growth. Of course, a book like this cannot tell the whole story, but I hope it will introduce the local church to some of the possibilities as the whole story is unfolded in the years ahead.

Let me reinforce my concern for spiritual formation by remarking that wherever we are now in our stage of spiritual growth, we must continue to grow as Christians. There are no limits to spiritual formation.

Emerson closed his essay on "Love" with these words: "We need not fear that we can lose anything by the progress of the soul, the soul may be trusted to the end. That which is so beautiful and attractive must be succeeded and supplemented only by what is more beautiful and so on forever."

Heraclitus wrote, "You cannot discover the boundaries of the soul by traveling in any direction." When the soul does actually progress and has its love fed and nourished by Divine Love, there are no human limits to its expansion and amplitude.

David Fleming, an American Jesuit, writes, "Spiritual direction has no limitations on it. We never totally outgrow it; and so it does not become outmoded according to the progress we have made in the spiritual life. The need is present throughout our lives because we are Christians who journey by faith."[1]

NOTE

[1] Jerome N. Neufelder and Mary C. Coelho, eds., *Writings on Spiritual Direction by Great Masters* (New York, Seabury, 1982), 56.

1

WHAT IS SPIRITUAL FORMATION?

The term "spiritual formation" has been given to us by the Roman Catholic Church. Across the centuries, in the training of priests, the Roman Catholic Church has always expressed a concern for the "priestly character" of its clergy and has included courses and training in spirituality in its ministerial curriculum.

While the priest-in-the-making was studying theology and other classical subjects and was learning the conduct of liturgies, masses, and sacraments, he was also being guided in the development of his own spiritual life. The ideal was personal spiritual development in conformity to spiritual models, being formed spiritually after the likeness of Christ.

When Roman Catholic seminaries became members of the accrediting association of theological schools in the United States, it was natural that they should continue "doing their thing." An increased emphasis on spirituality quickly surfaced. Soon theological seminaries, Protestant and Catholic alike, were sending representatives to conferences on spirituality, and the accrediting association established a special commission to deal with the spiritual life of seminarians. Rather quickly, and certainly providentially, this emphasis on spirituality caught fire on many seminary campuses, and spiritual formation plans were inaugurated.

In presenting this historical statement about renewed interest in spirituality, I do not wish to be misunderstood. I am not saying that Roman Catholics alone have emphasized spirituality in American Christianity. One of the keynotes in the Protestant Reformation was an insistence upon personal spiritual life as an evidence of justification by faith. As we shall see later, the genius of the Wesleyan Revival was spirituality. Every Protestant denomination has insisted upon a theology of the spiritual life. Most of the sectaries which have separated from major denominations have insisted upon a particular expression of spirituality as basic to Christian faith.

What I am saying, however, is that Protestant theological education in America in this century had largely neglected the formation of priestly character in theological education and had settled instead on imparting knowledge and skills. The academy had largely supplanted the chapel, even though both have traditionally characterized theological education. It took a new impetus from the outside to recall the seminaries to their full-orbed purposes in the training of ministers.

It is almost commonplace now to find a healthy emphasis upon spiritual formation on many theological seminary campuses. I believe, in the light of the evidence, that the fires of spiritual formation which are now beginning to burn on the altars of many denominations were ignited by the sparks of a renewed interest in spirituality from seminary campuses. This is not the usual direction of influence, but at least in this area theological seminaries have influenced the churches they serve to become more concerned about personal spirituality in the lives of their members.

What, then, do we mean by spiritual formation? Spirituality and spiritual formation belong together. "Being spiritual" has to do with one's sense of the sacred, the identification and affirmation of what one considers the supreme values in human existence. Spiritualality is the personal illustration of one's total commitment and loyalty to such supreme values. The quality of one's sense of the sacred determines the nature of one's spirituality. When we talk about spiritual formation we are speaking of the lived-out process of keeping spirituality transcendent in one's experience and life.

Many descriptive definitions of spiritual formation have been offered. Maxie Dunnam, who writes extensively in the area of spirituality, describes spiritual formation as "the dynamic process of receiving by faith and appropriating by commitment, discipline, and action, the living Christ into our lives to the end that our lives will conform to and manifest the living Christ in the world."

It is significant that the Academy for Spiritual Formation, sponsored by the Upper Room in Nashville, Tennessee, has adopted Dr. Dunnam's definition.

Teresa of Avila (1515–1582) was describing spiritual formation when she talked about "paying the Lord attention," and "keeping the Lord's house in order." Ignatius of Loyola (1491–1556) spoke of spiritual formation as fulfilling the goal of spirituality, which is to enable a Christian to become a contemplative in action.

Archdeacon Charles James Stranks, in his excellent volume, *Anglican Devotion,*[1] emphasizes that the purpose of spiritual formation is to "discover the plain way of holiness and walk therein," and that "the spiritually formed life is an ordered life of devotion, in which the vision of God, and the grace of God lead us into the fullest service of our fellowmen."

Spiritual formation leads to spiritual well-being which is the affirmation of life in a relationship with God, self, community, and environment that nurtures and celebrates wholeness.

During the academic year 1977–78, the Spiritual Formation Committee of Central Baptist Theological Seminary submitted the following statement concerning the meaning of spiritual formation:

> Spiritual Formation for the Christian is growth of the total person toward maturity in loving relationship to God, to self, to other persons in the community, and to the whole of God's created world.
>
> The goal is maximizing the use of God's gifts to a person in the journey toward wholeness.
>
> The process is the opening of the human spirit to the Holy Spirit at work in every dimension of human existence (cognitive, affective and physical) integrating all of life through the love and grace of Jesus Christ. The process is the forming of Christ in a human being.
>
> Spiritual Formation is growth in all relationships toward wholeness.

As excellent as the above definition is, I would like to add the word *relational* as a fourth "dimension of human existence," and "the power of the Holy Spirit" as a necessary integrating agent along with the "love and grace of Jesus Christ."

Norman Shawchuck, contemporary director of spiritual life for ministers, speaks of spiritual formation as "creating and sustaining for us a sense of New Testament reality revealed in Jesus Christ."

Spiritual formation is growth in holiness, employing the traditional means of spiritual devotion and discipline. It is "becoming a Christian" when a person already is one.

I was once asked on the spot to give a one-sentence definition of spiritual formation. Here was my response: "Spiritual formation is growth in spirituality according to the image of Christ."

But my favorite one-sentence description of spiritual formation is this: "It is the journey of the total person toward wholeness." This seems to say it all succinctly and accurately.

Spiritual formation is a *journey*. It is a dynamic process, always taking place, always progressing toward a desired spiritual objective, always manifesting evidence of personal and relational achievement. The spiritual life is never static; we are alive in Christ.

Spiritual formation is the journey of the *total person*. No longer do we restrict spirituality to an experience of the "soul." It relates to the total person, in all the areas and relationships of one's personality. Jesus talked about this centuries ago: "Love the Lord your God with all your heart [affectional] and with all your soul [spiritual] and with all your mind [rational] and with all your strength [physical] . . . [and] . . . your neighbor as yourself [relational]" (Mark 12:30–31).

Spiritual formation is the journey of the total person *toward wholeness*. God wills wholeness for all His creation. We are to be sanctified "wholly." The image of Christ is to be formed in us, so that we shall be "like Him."

Wholeness means (1) health, soundness, in every part of one's being; (2) the harmonious functioning of healthy parts within a unified personality; (3) the ability of each part of the person to fulfill its divinely appointed purpose.

Perhaps we can summarize what we are saying this way. Viewed *scripturally*, spiritual formation is growth in grace and in the knowledge of our Lord and Savior Jesus Christ. It is "gaining weight spiritually."

Theologically speaking, it is the process by which the image of Christ is formed in us. It is the process of reproduction within a person and among persons of the mind, spirit, character, and work of Jesus Christ. (See 2 Cor. 4:16, TEV.)

From a *psychological* perspective, spiritual formation is the pursuit of maturity.

To the one who understands *professional* processes, spiritual formation may be spoken of as development.

I have also been interested in the insights provided by local church people who have participated in seminars on spiritual formation. At Centenary Church in Lexington, the planning committee decided on the following one-sentence definition: "Spiritual formation is the intentional and systematic process of the opening of the total personality to the Holy Spirit in order to grow spiritually into the image of Christ."

At a nearby local church the people in one seminar suggested that spiritual formation meant (1) "becoming more Christian"; (2) "becoming 'the best,' 'the most,' person that God intends one to be"; (3) "learning to rest continually in God," using the biblical concept of "rest" as continuing dependency, trust, and appropriation of God's grace"; (4) "becoming increasingly attuned and responsive to God."

A missionary serving on an interdenominational church staff was present at an ecumenical seminar on spiritual formation which I conducted during the spring of 1984. When we were sharing various insights into the meaning of spiritual formation, he insisted that the Word of God be seen as prominent in the process. A few days after the seminar I received his suggested revision of one of the definitions we had considered as a group. I share it with you as a further insight into the meaning of spiritual formation: "The intentional and systematic process of growing into the image of Christ through obedience to the Scriptures by the power of the Holy Spirit in our total personality."

NOTE

[1] Charles James Stranks, *Anglican Devotion: Studies in the Spiritual Life of the Church of England Between the Reformation and the Oxford Movement* (London: SCM, 1961), 94–95.

2

THE BIBLICAL EMPHASIS

Spiritual formation is not a new discovery, even though the revival of interest in it is a contemporary spiritual phenomenon. The emphasis upon spiritual growth is the undertone, the tone, and the overtone of the Bible. It was the focus of the early church. It has been the impassioned concern of the saints of all ages as they have struggled with the tension between "the church of the Spirit" and "the church of authority." Every devotional classic of the centuries is a jeweled treatise on spiritual formation. Through the Christian centuries the *Te Deums* of "the glorious company of the apostles," of "the whole army of martyrs," of "the holy Church throughout all the world" have been expressed through spiritual experience and devotion. In our day, as we become concerned about spiritual growth, we are only rediscovering our neglected heritage as Christians.

Spiritual growth is one of the striking emphases of the Bible. As you read the Holy Scriptures with a sense of continuity, you become impressed by the ideal of growth into the image that God intended through the original creation and has made possible through the "new creation" in Jesus Christ.

The prophets remind us constantly that true life is possible only in conformity to God's revealed laws. Those who abide by God's words live; those who disregard the divine revelation perish. Life in the Scriptures is always spiritually dynamic— growing, developing, progressing toward a goal.

The book of Proverbs is replete with insights about how life is to be lived. Each proverb contains timeless truth, is based on real-life experience, and is morally and ethically sound. Proverbs is especially good for discipline, which is essential in the process of spiritual growth. Just about every personal discipline is mentioned by the wise writers of Proverbs. The secrets of disciplined living are unfolded in clear and unforgettable ways. Discipline is confirmed as one of the essentials in growth.

Were it possible, we could devote an entire chapter to the book of Psalms and the relation of its content to spiritual growth. The psalmists present aids to spiritual growth repeatedly and in a variety of ways. They insist again and again on the importance of prayer, the study of God's Word, worship, discipline, the keeping of one's vows, and concern for others.

The psalmists are, likewise, concerned about authentic introspection and a sobering evaluation of one's spiritual state. Listen to the psalmist as he prays:

> O Lord, thou hast searched me, and known me. . . . Whither shall I go from thy spirit? or whither shall I flee from thy presence . . . Search me, O God, and know my heart: try me, and know my thoughts: And see if there be any wicked way in me, and lead me in the way everlasting (Ps. 139:1, 7, 23–24, KJV).

In speaking about the emphasis upon spiritual growth in the Old Testament it can be noted that certain of the prophetic books, such as Isaiah, contain deeply moving insights about the nature of the spiritual life and its capacity for growth. We think at once of the "fear not" passages:

> Say to them that are of a fearful heart: Be strong, fear not; behold, your God. . .will come and save you (Isa. 35:4, KJV).
>
> Fear thou not; for I am with thee: be not dismayed; for I am thy God: I will strengthen thee; yea, I will uphold thee; yea, I will uphold thee with the right hand of my righteousness (Isa. 41:10, KJV).
>
> Fear not: for I have redeemed thee, I have called thee by thy name; thou art mine. When thou passest through the waters, I will be with thee; and through the rivers, they shall not overflow thee: when thou walkest through the fire, thou shalt not be burned; neither shall the flame kindle upon thee (Isa. 43:1, 2, KJV).

And how many times in our spiritual lives have we meditated upon and confided in those mighty words with which the fortieth chapter of Isaiah's prophecy ends:

> He giveth power to the faint; and to them that have no might he increaseth strength. . . .They that wait upon the LORD shall renew their strength; they shall mount up with wings as eagles; they shall run, and not be weary; and they shall walk, and not faint (Isa. 40:29, 31, KJV).

When we turn to the New Testament, it may properly be said that growth toward wholeness is a basic theme. Jesus Christ was an example of symmetrical growth. He increased in wisdom and stature and in favor with God and man. Among the many disciplines that Jesus practiced were setting priorities, the devotional life, self-control, servanthood, and persistence.

Especially significant were Jesus' devotional disciplines. He affirmed constantly the transcendence of spirituality over material things. He practiced prayer and worship. He studied the Scriptures. He sought always to be fully obedient to His Father's will. Study carefully His life and ministry. He took time to be holy; He practiced those devotional disciplines which contributed to His holiness; and His life manifested the Divine Image.

In His teachings Jesus insisted upon the totality of devotion and discipline. He said that the greatest commandment is to love God with all one's heart and mind and soul and strength. He was repeatedly talking about life—spiritual life, growing life, abundant life.

In the early church, evangelism, experience, and expression were blended harmoniously. People needed to be evangelized so that they might experience the redeeming grace of God in Christ. But then they were to grow in the grace and the knowledge of the Lord Jesus Christ (2 Peter 3:18).

The apostle Paul wrote often about spiritual growth—his own personal growth and that of those to whom he wrote. Speaking personally, he wrote to his beloved Philippians, "Not that I have already obtained this or am already perfect; but I press on. . .to what lies ahead. . .toward the goal for the prize of the upward call of God in Christ Jesus" (Phil. 3:12–14, RSV).

For the Ephesians Paul prayed that they might "[speak] the truth in love. . .grow up in every way into him who is the head, into Christ" (Eph. 4:15, RSV); "to mature manhood, to the measure of the stature of the fulness of Christ" (Eph. 4:13, RSV).

Paul shared the secret of spiritual growth with the Corinthians:

> All of us, then, reflect the glory of the Lord with uncovered faces; and that same glory, coming from the Lord who is the Spirit, transforms us into His likeness, in an even greater degree of glory (2 Cor. 3:18, TEV).

The apostle was just as concerned about the spiritual growth of the Christians in Galatia and in Colosse:

> Just like a mother in childbirth, I feel the same kind of pain for you, until Christ's nature is formed in you (Gal. 4:19, TEV).
>
> So we preach Christ to all men. We warn and teach everyone, with all possible wisdom, in order to bring each one into God's presence as a mature individual in union with Christ (Col. 1:28, TEV).

The apostle Peter began his second epistle with a passionate plea for spiritual growth:

> Do your best to *add* goodness to your faith; to your goodness *add* knowledge; to your knowledge *add* self-control; to your self-control *add* endurance; to your endurance *add* godliness; to your godliness *add* brotherly love; and to your brotherly love *add* love (2 Peter 1:5–7, TEV, emphasis mine).

The apostle John, both in his gospel and his epistles, provides insights about spiritual growth. John speaks often of abiding, of bringing forth "fruit," "more" fruit, even "much" fruit. He writes about manifesting our faith through our love and good works. It is John who is confident that through the power of God we can be successful in our spiritual growth, for he says that when we shall see Christ, we shall be like Him (1 John 3:2).

In the light of the scriptural evidence it is little wonder that spiritual formation has been the heartbeat of sanctity across the Christian centuries. In his *Confessions* St. Augustine (354–430) paid tribute to his saintly mother, Monica, for her prayers that Christ might be born within him and after such a spiritual birth, the image of Christ might be formed within him.

William Law (1686–1761) set forth Christian salvation as consisting in nothing less than the birth and life within a human soul of our Savior Jesus Christ. Law declares that He who was born for us and died for us may be born again within us and live His life in our life. He bids his readers write this upon their hearts, that our salvation lies in this alone, the manifestation of the nature, life, and spirit of Jesus Christ in our inward person.

Had we the time to call the roll of the saints and study their writings, the conclusion about the imperative of spiritual formation would be universal. (For illustration of such a roll, read through the names listed in the table of contents of Thomas Kepler's monumental anthology, *The Fellowship of the Saints* now published under the title *An Anthology of Devotional Literature*.)[1]

Many of us are hearing a lot about the Wesleyan quadrilateral these days—the testing of religious truth by Scripture, tradition, experience, and reason. When we apply this fourfold test to what we are considering in these pages, the verdict is clear and convincing: growth is the norm for spiritual experience and life.

NOTE

[1] Thomas Kepler, *An Anthology of Devotional Literature* (Nashville: Abingdon, 1948).

3

THE WESLEYAN WAY

The Wesleyan Revival of the eighteenth century had a significant influence on Christian spiritual formation, and Christian historians affirm that an emphasis upon spirituality was the genius of the Methodist movement. Michael Ramsey, former archbishop of Canterbury, declared that among the priceless gifts which Methodists can contribute to Anglicans is the focus upon holiness and assurance.

Until his Aldersgate experience in 1738, John Wesley had learned all he knew about spirituality from other people. After 1738, by the grace of God, he generated his own spirituality and people began to learn from him.

Both John and Charles Wesley discovered that spirituality is not something which is cultivated as a merely human process. Their conversions in 1738 made them realize that the very possibility of spirituality is the free gift of God. But then God has established ways and means for us to receive it and let it develop and mature in our lives. This is spiritual formation.

That John Wesley should emphasize spiritual growth seems inevitable when we consider the fact that as a child he was reared in an atmosphere of spirituality. His mother, Susanna Wesley, was the dominant spiritual influence in the rectory at Epworth. Until the end of her life John sat at her knee.

Susanna's program of home education was designed not only to give a child a broad background of general knowledge, but to instill a deep sense of reverence and a desire for spiritual development. When John, whom she called "Jacky," was five, she began his education. In one day he learned the alphabet, as did the other children. She taught him to spell from the first chapter of the Old Testament: "In the beginning God created the heavens and the earth. . . ." After three months, five-year-old John could read as well as many educated adults.

Through their early years and into their teens, Susanna educated her children in the home, six hours a day plus one evening to each child in rotation. She recorded her plan:

> I resolved to begin with my own children. . . .I observe the following method: I take such a proportion of time as I can share, every night, to discourse with each child apart. On Monday I talk with Molly, on Tuesday with Hetty, Wednesday with Nancy, Thursday with Jacky, Friday with Patty, Saturday with Charles and with Emilia and Sukey together on Sunday.[1]

To the end of his life, John Wesley never forgot those evenings with his mother.

The home school always opened and closed with the singing of a psalm. Susanna planned well the course of studies. When John emerged from Epworth he had a solid background in literature, science, languages, and logic as well as in religious matters.

Susanna Wesley was a strict disciplinarian. A study of her life and teaching procedures reveals that she established such rules as the following for keeping her children in the paths of righteousness:

1. Eating between meals not allowed.
2. As children, they are to be in bed by 8 P.M.
3. They are required to take medicine without complaining.
4. Subdue self-will in a child, and thus work together with God to save the child's soul.
5. Teach a child to pray as soon as he can speak.
6. Require all to be still during family worship.
7. Give them nothing they cry for, and only that which they ask for politely.
8. To prevent lying, punish no fault which is first confessed and repented.
9. Never allow a sinful act to go unpunished.

10. Never punish a child twice for a single offense.

11. Commend and reward good behaviour.

12. Any attempt to please, even if poorly performed should be commended.

13. Preserve property rights, even in the smallest matters.

14. Strictly observe all promises.

15. Require no daughter to work before she can read well.

16. Teach children to fear the Lord.

Despite her many household duties Susanna Wesley kept faithfully her own times for prayer, meditation, and writing. John testified to her methodical and persistent nature when he wrote, "She never suffered anything to break in upon her stated hours of retirement, which she sacredly observed from the age of 17 or 18 to 72."

So John Wesley came to adulthood and even into church ordination very much aware of the significance of spiritual devotion and discipline. When you observe the early spiritual quests of both Wesleys, you cannot fail to notice their reliance upon the means of grace and spiritual ministries as the hope for fulfilling their longing for personal spiritual satisfaction. The Holy Club at Lincoln College, Oxford, which met in John's rooms in the early 1730s, was a form of corporate spiritual formation. The unsuccessful missionary journey to Georgia (1736–38) was intended to enhance spiritual growth. In their fellowship with the Moravians they sought advice and guidance from spiritual directors.

Certainly nothing that John Wesley did from a spiritual motivation before Aldersgate was ever lost. But his Aldersgate experience (May 24, 1738) exposed the fallacy that spiritual growth can be effective apart from an assured experience of spiritual birth. Theoretically he had been exposed to spiritual formation from his earliest childhood. After 1738 he became an authentic participant in the process.

The Wesleyan emphasis upon the new birth naturally led to a focus on the new life. Once life appears, something has to be done about it. After birth, life either grows or perishes. It is just as true in the spiritual realm. Spiritual life begins with experience of the new birth, but it does not end there. Actually, if it does end there, it ends.

Dr. Steve Harper, in his book *John Wesley's Message for Today,* has a chapter entitled "Don't Stop Now." The chapter is a summary statement of Wesley's insistence upon growth in grace as the norm in spiritual experience.[2] Wesley continually reminded his followers that growth in grace is not accidental or automatic. Rather it is a spiritual process in which the Christian must choose to participate. He is explicit in his conviction that growth in grace always occurs through the means of grace which God has established. (This will be discussed in more detail later in the chapter.)

Wesley conceived of spiritual growth as a chief ingredient in spiritual worship. In expounding the Scripture passage about loving God with all one's heart, soul, mind, and strength, he wrote:

> A third thing we are to understand by serving God, is, to *resemble,* or *imitate* him.
>
> So the ancient father said: *Optimus Dei cultus, imitari quem colis: "It is the best worship or service to God, to imitate him you worship."*[3]

John Wesley's "order of salvation" lays great emphasis upon nurture and spiritual growth. Consider this progression in Wesley's theology of salvation:

> Prevenient grace—convicting grace—repentance and faith—saving grace—assurance—sanctification begun—growth in grace—the "event" of entire sanctification—assurance—continued growth in "perfection"—glorification.

In reference to the Christian's motivation for spiritual formation, Wesley provides a distinctive insight when he concludes that we grow in grace out of a sense of assurance.

Wesley had a meaningful devotional life. Being human as we are, it was not perfect, but in many ways it was exemplary and provides numerous insights for us in our spiritual growth. Professor Steve Harper, whose doctoral thesis was on the devotional life of John Wesley (Duke Divinity School), gives a four-fold characterization of Wesley's practice. It was realistic. He profited by his mistakes. It was disciplined. His basic intention to relate himself to God on a personal basis never wavered throughout his entire Christian life. It had great breadth. Even though he was "a man of one Book"—the Bible—he drew on Anglican, Puritan, Moravian, and Roman Catholic sources for devotional support. He was influenced by such devotional masters as Henry Scougal, Lorenzo Scupoli, Lewis Bayly, Richard Allestree, Henry Hammond, Jeremy Taylor, William Law, Thomas à Kempis, Francois Fénelon, and the *Theologia Germanica*. And, fourth, Wesley's devotional life always had a community dimension. He never allowed his spiritual life to deteriorate into a private religion. He was constantly sharing with others. If the Roman Catholic–Anglican tradition was insisting "no salvation without the church," Wesley would add "and no spiritual development apart from the church." Wesley's remark that he knew of no holiness save social holiness is often repeated.

Wesley was an extremely disciplined person, which contributed significantly to his spiritual growth. His disciplines included sleep, exercise, food, and raiment.

He was disciplined about time and money. During his Oxford days he wrote, "Leisure and I have taken leave of each other." His advice about money was "Make all you can; save all you can; give all you can."

He was disciplined in his study life. His chair at his City Road house in London was made so that he could sit astride it like the saddle in which he spent so much time. On it there was a reading board, writing arm, and a place for books. The chaise in which he traveled was closed on one side to provide a place for shelves of books.

He was disciplined in prayer. He had a prayer room at his City Road house that he visited regularly early in the morning, "without exception." In 1728 he prepared for himself an extensive prayer manual to be followed in his devotional life. Wesley knew that one's devotional life cannot be based on emotions. It must be centered in one's will. The Christian knows what is right and must do it. Discipline becomes the key which keeps one's spiritual life going through fair weather and foul.

Wesley's concern for the spiritual formation of new converts was revealed in his organized structure to conserve the fruits of his preaching. He organized converts into societies and within the societies created smaller groups known as classes and bands.

John Wesley prepared a careful set of General Rules to

govern the societies. These General Rules were addressed to an association of Christians committed to helping one another live the Christian life.

To enter one of Wesley's societies was easy, requiring only a sincere intention to be saved. But to continue in the societies one's life had to change, since the sincerity of one's desire would show itself by the fruit of Christian behavior. Three times in Wesley's Rules he says, "It is therefore expected of all who continue therein that they shall continue to evidence their desire of salvation—by avoiding evil, doing good, and observing the practices of Christian piety."

Any student of Wesleyan insights into spiritual formation should study in depth Wesley's General Rules, which appear in each quadrennial edition of *The Book of Discipline of the United Methodist Church.*

Classes consisted of groups of twelve, each with its own appointed leader. The groups met together each week, and attendance was compulsory. The leader conducted a public examination into the manner of life of each member of the class, to praise those who were living well, to admonish those who were falling before temptation, and to exhort all to go on in the way of holiness.

Also, every week the leader of a class personally visited every class member. "How's it going," the class leader would ask privately, "with you and the Lord? With your family? With you and other Methodists? With your friends and neighbors?"

The classes offered early Methodists a laboratory for a personal experience of the gospel.

Wesley was prone to prepare lists of questions by which Methodists could examine their spiritual state. Here is a sampling of some of those questions:

> Is the love of God shed abroad in my heart? Has any sin, inward or outward, dominion over me?
>
> What known sins have I committed since I last met with others?
>
> What particular temptations have I met with?
>
> How was I delivered?
>
> Do I really desire others to tell me what they think, fear, and hear concerning me?

Have I mentioned any failing or fault of any man when it was not necessary for the good of another?

Have I unnecessarily grieved anyone by word or deed?

Have I desired the praise of men?

Have I set apart some time for endeavoring after a lively sense of the sufferings of Christ and my own sins?

Have I resumed my claim to my body, soul, friends, fame, or fortune, which I have made over to God; or repented of my gift, when God accepted any of them at my hands?

Have I said anything with stern look, accent or gesture, particularly with regard to religion?[4]

Sometimes bands were also set up within the societies. These were generally organized according to sex, and were designed to make possible an examination of life even more intimate than could be secured in the meetings of the classes.

How true is the comment that Wesley gathered believers through his preaching but nurtured them through the societies. Evangelism for Wesley was more than proclamation. He not only wanted to *get people,* but to *keep* people.

Wesley recognized the need for fellowship to assure accountability. Such a genius for organizing Christians into nurturing groups assured the continuance of the eighteenth-century evangelical revival. But he never allowed the societies to become substitute churches. He found his place in the regular worship of the Church of England, and he intended that his followers would do the same.

John Wesley placed a great emphasis upon the necessity of utilizing the means of grace for spiritual growth. He wrote, "Beware. . .of imagining you shall obtain the End, without using the means conducive to it." For Wesley there are five chief means of grace: prayer, the Word, fasting, Christian conference or fellowship, and the Lord's Supper. Even though all these were tremendously important for both John and Charles Wesley, the Lord's Supper was always the means of grace par excellence. He wrote:

> Of these Blessings CHRIST from above is pleased to bestow sometimes more, sometimes less, in the several Ordinances of his Church, which as the Stars of Heaven, differ from each other in Glory. *Fasting, Prayer, Hearing,* his word, are all good Vessels, to draw Water from this Well of Salvation. But they are not equal. The

Holy Communion when well used, exceeds as much in Blessings, as it exceeds in danger of a Curse, when wickedly and irreverently taken.[5]

In a very real sense, John Wesley was a spiritual director to early Methodists. He provided such spiritual direction through (1) his organization of Methodists into societies, classes, and bands; (2) his preaching; (3) his "conferences" and conversations; (4) his extensive correspondence; (5) his spiritual dialogues at annual conferences; (6) his writings.

Wesley's counsels and instructions concerning spiritual growth are numerous and specific. He wrote in *A Plain Account of Christian Perfection:*

1. Watch and pray continually against pride.

2. Beware of that daughter of pride, enthusiasm (heated imagination which is quick to ascribe everything to God).

3. Beware of antinomianism, making void the law, or any part of it through faith.

4. Beware of sins of commission; lose no opportunity of doing good in any kind.

5. Beware of desiring anything but God.

6. Beware of schism, of making a rent in the Church of Christ.

7. Be exemplary in all things: particularly in outward things (as in dress), in little things, in the laying out of your money (avoiding every needless expense) in deep, steady seriousness, and in the solidity and usefulness of all your conversation.

For the benefit of the Methodists, John Wesley published a *Collection of Forms of Prayer for Every Day in the Week* (1733). In 1735 he published *A New Translation of à Kempis' Imitation of Christ.* As a part of the Preface to this abridgment, he gives timely advice on spiritual reading, addressed particularly to those "who, knowing they have not yet attained, are already perfect, mind this one thing, and pressing toward the work, despise no assistance which is offered them. . . ."

He also published during the years 1749–55 a Christian library of forty volumes under the title, *The Best of Practical Divinity.* This contained the writings from the early church Fathers all the way to the time of Wesley's contemporaries.

This chapter on the Wesleyan way of spiritual formation

would be incomplete without some reference to the hymns of Charles Wesley. Among the more than six thousand hymns authored by "the poet of Methodism" are numerous hymns whose content is focused on spiritual growth. Just as studies in depth have been made of Wesley's hymns on initial salvation, Christian perfection, the church and the sacraments, so an extensive research could be done into what Charles wrote about the process of achieving the holy life.

Even a small sampling from his hymns ought to whet our spiritual appetites.

> Leave no unguarded place,
>   No weakness of the soul,
> Take ev'ry virtue, ev'ry grace,
>   And fortify the whole.
>
> From strength to strength go on,
>   Wrestle and fight and pray,
> Tread all the powers of darkness down
>   And win the well-fought day.[6]

* * *

> I want a principle within
>   Of watchful, godly fear,
> A sensibility of sin,
>   A pain to feel it near
>
> Help me the first approach to feel
>   Of pride or wrong desire,
> To catch the wanderings of my will,
>   And quench the kindling fire.[7]

* * *

> Arm me with jealous care,
>   As in thy sight to live,
> And O, thy servant, Lord, prepare,
>   A strict account to give!
>
> Help me to watch and pray,
>   And on thyself rely,
> Assured, if I my trust betray,
>   I shall forever die.[8]

* * *

> . . .Give me on thee to wait,
>   Till I can all things do . . .
>
> I want a sober mind,
>   A self-renouncing will. . . .
>
> I want a godly fear,
>   A quick discerning eye. . . .
>
> I want a true regard,
>   A single steady aim,
> Unmoved by threatening or reward,
>   To thee and thy great name;
> A jealous, just concern
>   For thine, immortal praise. . . .[9]

*   *   *

> Help us to help each other, Lord,
>   Each other's cross to bear;
> Let us each his friendly aid afford,
>   And feel his brother's care.[10]

*   *   *

> He bids us build each other up,
>   And, gathered into one,
> To our high calling's glorious hope,
>   We hand in hand go on.[11]

The Wesleyan emphasis upon the experience of heart holiness and the holy life is indissolubly linked with spiritual formation. Holiness means the forming of the image of Christ within. This is possible only through the process of spiritual growth. God provides the possibility: "God is at work in you" to accomplish His will. But we must so respond that the possible becomes actual: "Work out your own salvation with fear and trembling" (Phil. 2:12–13, RSV).

There is a growing realization that Wesley's concepts on spiritual formation have both relevance and potency for today. He saw personal devotions as a basic generative powerhouse of religious experience. He studied the Scriptures. He had his own patterns of prayer. He held to the practice of taking Holy Communion regularly, usually at least twice a week. He recognized the practicality of the small group for spiritual growth, and he utilized the power of group participation as an instrument for maturing personality in association with others.

One of my esteemed friends in the Christian ministry is the Rev. Dr. David Waite Yohn, long-time pastor of the West Parish in West Barnstable, Massachusetts, the oldest Congregational church in continuous worship in the world. He was a student of and participant in spiritual formation long before he discovered John Wesley. But in his doctoral studies he confronted Wesleyan thought and practices intimately for the first time. Immediately he became aware of the viability of the Wesleyan approach to spirituality. He told how he had found in Wesleyanism "a beautiful schema for spiritual formation." He commented, "John Wesley offers a dynamic, progressive spiritual principle beginning with new life in Christ and continually going on unto perfection."

NOTES

[1] Maldwyn Edwards, *Family Circle: A Study of the Epworth Household in Relation to John and Charles Wesley* (London: Epworth, 1949), 68.

[2] Steve Harper, *John Wesley's Message for Today* (Grand Rapids: Zondervan/Francis Asbury Press, 1983).

[3] Al Bryant, *The John Wesley Reader* (Waco, Tex.: Word, 1983), 100.

[4] Albert Outler, *John Wesley* (New York: Oxford, 1964), 180ff.

[5] John Wesley and Charles Wesley, *Hymns on the Lord's Supper* (Bristol: Felix Farley, c. 1745).

[6] "Soldiers of Christ, Arise."

[7] "I Want a Principle Within."

[8] "A Charge to Keep I Have."

[9] "Jesus, My Strength, My Hope."

[10] "Jesus, United by Thy Grace."

[11] "All Praise to Our Redeeming Lord."

4

THE IMPERATIVES OF SPIRITUAL FORMATION

In previous chapters we looked at the biblical case for and the Wesleyan tradition of spiritual formation. Now we will take yet another approach. The Christian life makes certain demands upon us, and I want to look at several of these and demonstrate how we must be engaged in spiritual formation if we are to live up to our obligations as Christians.

We will look at the following eleven obligations of the Christian life that require of us the discipline and practice of spiritual formation.

1. Christians need to become more Christlike.
2. Christians need to grow spiritually or they will perish.
3. Christians need to struggle against evil.
4. Christians need to discover their true selves.
5. Christians need a proper balance between mind and emotions.
6. Christians need an inner strength to face life's difficulties.
7. Christians need to be engaged in redemptive ministries.
8. Christians need a renewable inner strength so they can serve others.
9. Christians need a proper balance between the material and the spiritual.
10. Christians need a balance between a focus on themselves and a focus on the common life.

11. Christians need to recover a sense of the personal in their faith and guard it against the blights of institutionalism and rationalism.

Let's look at each of these in more detail.

Christians need to become more Christlike

Spiritual formation is imperative for the Christian to fulfill the divine ideal of being Christlike. It is God's intention for us—through both the original creation and the re-creation made possible by Jesus Christ—that the image of Jesus Christ be formed within us. The primary purpose of the Christian faith is that we know Christ and become like Him.

Spiritual knowledge involves obedience; spiritual union involves imitation. Jesus called His disciples that they might be with Him and consequently become like Him. Previously we made reference to John Wesley's conviction that the imitation of Christ is the Christian's chief worship.

Already we have noted that spiritual formation was the primary objective of the ministries of the early church, that spiritual formation has been the heartbeat of Christian sanctity across the centuries, and that the Wesleyan movement has traditionally emphasized spiritual formation as an indispensable element in its concept of spirituality.

Spiritual formation confirms the conclusion that the emphasis of the Christian faith is on *being* as requisite for *doing*. Writing to the Corinthians, St. Paul declared that "we show that we are God's servants" by our character (2 Cor. 6:4, TEV).

Miguel de Molinos (1640–1697) wrote, "The perfection of the soul consists not in speaking, nor in thinking much on God, but in loving him sufficiently."[1]

In contrast to the world's primary emphasis upon *doing*, God's emphasis is on *being*. "He hath chosen us . . . before the foundation of the world, that we should *be* holy and without blame before him in love" (Eph. 1:4, KJV). To those who receive Christ God gives power to *become* the sons of God (John 1:12). God's purpose for His church is to sanctify it and cleanse it and some day to present it to Himself, without spot or wrinkle, holy and without blemish (Eph. 5:26–27). Jesus was always emphasizing the significance of *being*. In the Beatitudes He kept saying, "blessed *are* . . . ." To all the disciples He said, "I will make you to *become* fishers of men" (Mark 1:17, KJV) and "Ye shall *be* witnesses unto me" (Acts 1:8, KJV).

The Christian's primary witness is in the area of personal spiritual character. Some of us remember those days in the early grades of public school when we used to line up each month to be weighed on the scales in the principal's office. There was a little boy in such a line who wanted to weigh more than the boy ahead of him. So he proceeded to blow up and puff out his cheeks with air. But another boy, seeing what he was doing, said to him, "That will do you no good; you can weigh only what you are."

Many people will see Christ only through the lives of those who profess to love Him. In 1935 when King George V and Queen Mary of Great Britain celebrated their twenty-fifth anniversary on the throne, an interesting thing happened during the gigantic parade. Many folks on the back rows of the seats along the line of march and those standing on side streets could get a glimpse of the royal couple only as they looked into mirrors held high above the crowd. So in preparation for the parade, people everywhere were seen polishing their mirrors.

This is an applicable analogy to Christians today. The only glimpse many people will ever have of the Kings of kings is through the reflection of Him portrayed in the lives of His believing followers. So Christians must keep their mirrors polished.

To use another analogy, when a TV set is first delivered and put into service, the image is sharp and clear as it was intended to be. But when disturbing influences come into play or any part of the mechanism gets out of kilter, the picture can become blurred and unsteady. The original image is distorted. An expert is needed who can restore the image to its original perfection. As he goes to work on the TV set, making an adjustment here and there, the image becomes clearer and clearer.

Spiritually speaking, this is the meaning of spiritual formation. The image of God in us became distorted and must be restored. Such restoration is possible only through the forming of the image of Christ within us. God is the expert. We respond to all of the adjustments that He makes.

But it must be kept in mind that the purpose of *being* is always for *doing*. Even though we can do no more than we are, as we become we do. Growth in spiritual life leads inevitably to activity in the name of Jesus Christ.

Take the illustration of Peter and John who healed the crippled man at the Beautiful Gate of the Temple (Acts 4). Even their enemies recognized that their power came from their having been with Jesus (v. 13).

One of the significant recent books on prayer is Miriam Murphy's volume, *Prayer in Action*.[2] Even though most of the book is devoted to a study of the nature of prayer and a presentation of techniques for a satisfying prayer life, the underlying thesis is that effective prayer always manifests itself in action. Centuries ago Ignatius Loyola spoke about the normal Christian being "a contemplative in action," and John Wesley declared, as I noted earlier, that he knew of no holiness except social holiness.

All of this has relevance to the local church today. When the church recognizes spiritual formation as the divine norm, it pays more attention to its responsibility for contributing to the process of spiritual maturity.

It will also help the local church gain a correct understanding of the relationship between evangelism and spiritual formation. Evangelism is not the sole objective of the church's program. The primary ministry of the church is spiritual formation. When professing Christians are growing spiritually they will become effective evangelists. Any attempts at evangelism apart from spiritually vital and motivated "evangelists," will prove fruitless in the end.

Christians need to grow spiritually or they will perish

Spiritual formation is imperative because spiritual life conforms to the law of all life: grow or perish. There is nothing static in life. Life is dynamic. It either grows or dies. In the same way, spiritual life either progresses or regresses.

Frank Laubach was aware of this when he wrote, "I have no temptations now to do wrong, but only to slump into a sluggish, stupid goodness." One is reminded of John Wesley's comment about those who were "fast asleep in the dead form of godliness."[3]

Baron Friedrich von Hugel wrote, "The soul is—maintaining its life always by a continual re-constitution, by effort, strength, temptation, growth and new levels and starting points. . . ."[4]

It is a law of the universe that the best things are seldom seen in their best form. The ideal of perfection is always present, but continuous growth is essential to approximate it more and more.

Von Hugel also writes that the formation of character is a process by which our spiritual substance moves from being potentially moral to becoming actually so. It is a succession of acts by which we gradually, but always only by ever-fresh acts, change our possibilities into actualities and again use the resultants as so many possibilities for fresh acts and achievements. This is a difficult concept for us because we tend to think of character as being static rather than dynamic. Yet the soul is not only an energizing substance; it is itself constituted by that continuous action of God's work within the soul and the soul's work in God.[5]

We remind ourselves of the emphasis of the Holy Scriptures upon growth as the secret of spiritual life:

> The path of the righteous is as the shining light, that shineth more and more unto the perfect day (Prov. 4:18, KJV).
> Not that I have already obtained this or am already perfect; but I press on (Phil. 3:12, RSV).
> Until we all attain. . .to mature manhood, to the measure of the stature of the fulness of Christ (Eph. 4:13, RSV).
> This I pray, that your love may abound yet more and more in knowledge and in all judgment (Phil. 1:9, KJV).
> My little children, with whom I am again in travail until Christ be formed in you (Gal. 4:19, RSV).
> You . . . must be perfect, as your heavenly Father is perfect (Matt. 5:48).
> [We warn] every man, and [teach] every man in all wisdom; that we may present every man perfect in Christ (Col. 1:28, KJV).

Christians need to struggle against evil

Spiritual formation is imperative because the Christian life in this present world is a continuous struggle against evil.

D. L. Moody wrote:

> When I was converted, I made this mistake: I thought the battle was already mine, the victory already won, the crown already in my grasp. I thought the old things had passed away, that all things had

become new, and that my old corrupt nature, the old life, was gone. But I found out, after serving Christ for a few months, that conversion was only like enlisting in the army—that there was a battle on hand.

John Wesley warned Christians about the innumerable foes which assault them and seek to destroy them. In one brief passage alone he mentions "a thousand temptations," "ten thousand more," "temptations from good men," "from an evil world," "secret, sworn eternal foes," "our adversary the devil," "his infernal legions."[6]

Wesley continually reminded the Methodists that there was never a moment in their spiritual lives when they could get along without the overcoming power of the grace of God. Backsliding was always attributed to the fact that a professing Christian failed to realize the serious nature of the Christian life and began trusting in his own strength alone.

Isaac Watts penned these lines which we have sung often:

> Are there no foes for me to face?
>   Must I not stem the flood?
> Is this vile world a friend to grace,
>   To help me on to God?
>
> Sure I must fight, if I would reign;
>   Increase my courage, Lord. . . .

This is what Paul was saying centuries before to the Ephesians:

> Be strong in the Lord and in his mighty power. Put on the full armor of God so that you can take your stand against the devil's schemes. For our struggle is not against flesh and blood, but against the rulers, against the authorities, against the powers of this dark world and against the spiritual forces of evil in the heavenly realms. Therefore put on the full armor of God, so that when the day of evil comes, you may be able to stand your ground, and after you have done everything, to stand (Eph. 6:10–13, NIV).

Christians need to discover their true selves

Spiritual formation is imperative so we can discover our authentic selves. There is a universal need for self-discovery; far too many people go through life wearing masks. It is easier to put on a show than it is to sit and listen to one's conscience. People get excited—about the detached and impersonal—but not about that which is personal and inward. People seek to construct bubbles around themselves to shield themselves from the real and authentic.

Boris Pasternak writes in *Doctor Zhivago,* "Oh, how one wishes sometimes to escape from the meaningless dullness of human eloquence, from all those sublime phrases, to take refuge in nature, so inarticulate."

The March 3, 1980, issue of *Time* had a cover story about the actor Peter Sellers. Appearing on the Muppet Show, he was told by Kermit the Frog that it was all right to "just relax and be yourself," to which Sellers replied, "I could never be myself. You see, there is no me. I do not exist."[7]

Speaking of human personality in general, power comes only through authenticity. The January 1983 issue of *Reader's Digest* contained an article entitled "The Awesome Power to Be Ourselves," by Ardis Whitman.[8] The thesis of the article is that authenticity is the secret of influential personality power. Here are some of the statements of the author:

> [Speaking of individuals who have helped to change society]—they all spoke and acted themselves, resolutely standing up for what they believed. . .they were "authentic."
>
> Authenticity proceeds from the center of a person's life, but is not self-centered. . . .
>
> Socrates taught that to "know thyself" is the basis of all knowledge; Shakespeare wrote, "To thine own self be true. . .thou canst not then be false to any man."
>
> Authenticity makes each person's life count by restoring power to the individual. . . .Authentic people recognize the direction in which their lives are meant to go. . . .
>
> The authentic person does not dissipate energy in contradictions. . . .
>
> As with the splitting of the atom, the opening of the self gives us access to a hidden power. It comes with feeling at home with oneself and therefore at home in the universe. It is the greatest power in all the world—the power to be ourselves.

It is especially true in the realm of the spirit that to experience spiritual power, we must discover our authentic self. George Herbert, English poet (1593–1632), wrote, "By all means use sometime to be alone, salute thyself; see what thy soul doth wear.

Dare to look in thy chest, for 'tis thy own; and tumble up and down what thou findest there."

Thomas Merton, the modern monk who excelled in the inner search, believed that the problem of sanctity and salvation is in fact the problem of finding out "who I am and of discovering my true self." On one occasion he declared, "If we have chosen the way of falsity, we must not be surprised that truth eludes us when we finally come to need it."

A study of writings on spiritual direction across the centuries reveals the necessity of honesty in dealing with one's own spiritual state. Time and time again, for illustration, Baron Friedrich von Hugel, prominent spiritual director, confesses his own needs in his letters. He writes: "Our service of God really means for us the fighting of self."[9]

When you have discovered your identity, you need to say little else. Toyohiko Kagawa, the Japanese Christian who spent his life working with and for the poor, was speaking at Princeton. When he finished his talk, one student said to another, "He didn't say much, did he?" A woman sitting nearby leaned over and murmured, "When you're hanging on a cross, you don't have to say anything."

Authenticity has both its negative and positive aspects. Negatively, it means taking off the masks, resolving the inner conflict in personality, identifying the true selves within oneself and insisting that the bad selves go. Positively, it is the experience of inner unity, the end of doublemindedness, and the discovery of the true "collected" person. The "uncollected" person is pressed for time, hates silence, is restless, is anxious about circumstances, and is really too busy to live and love. The "collected" person is just the opposite. Authenticity is the character of the "collected person." The psalmist prayed, "Unite my heart to fear thy name."

Self-discovery reveals to us our potential when illumined, cleansed, and heightened by the grace of God. So spiritual formation becomes the stimulus to the development of the discovered self. Spiritual energies are required, for as Frederick William Faber reminds us, "to be straightforward with God is neither an easy nor a common grace."

Roman Catholic Archbishop Joseph Bernardin has written that honest Christians will admit that they spend much of their time pretending, but that when they are in the presence of God in prayer, they have candidly to own up to their strengths and weaknesses and total dependence on God.

So spiritual formation becomes a means of pursuing successfully the struggle for self-affirmation, self-definition, and autonomous self-donation.

Christians need a proper balance between mind and emotions

Spiritual formation is imperative to establish and maintain a proper balance between the emotions and the mind in Christian experience. Seemingly there has always been a tension between these two areas of human personality. The ancient Hebrews believed the heart to be the all-important component in one's relationship to God. When the "Great Commandment" appears in the Mosaic literature, "mind" is omitted from the delineation of the totality of one's love for God. It was Jesus who included "mind" in his restatement of the commandment. He said, in effect, "You are to love God not only with your heart (emotions), spirit (soul), and strength (body), but also with your mind (intellect)" (Mark 12:30).

This tension between mind and emotions has been evident across the Christian centuries. The purely rationalistic approach to religious experience has stood in stark contrast to the primarily emotional approach. So both philosophers and theologians have often been classified either by their intellectual or their emotional approach to the validity of personal experience.

Strangely enough, advances in religion have often resulted from a reaction to one or other of these basic approaches. John Wesley's emphasis upon personal spiritual experience was a reaction to "the age of reason," in which the rationalistic theology of deism was prominent. On the other hand, Jonathan Edwards' theology, while never minimizing religious experience, insisted upon the rationality of the faith.

Recent years on the religion scene have witnessed a strange interplay between mind and emotion in religion. The renaissance of evangelical theology has continually focused on the converted, sanctified mind, sensitive to the divine revelation. On the other hand, many of the revival groups appearing in evangelicalism have staked their major claims on personal feeling and emotion.

We cannot elaborate on this issue here, but it needs to be said that so-called "intellectual spirituality" apart from warm emotional responses to God becomes sterile and fruitless. On the other hand, no spiritual experience or activity, however valid, can be sustained permanently without a wholesome theological undergirding.

John Wesley struggled personally with this tension of the relation of mind and emotion in religion. He confessed that what might be called "peak experiences," as far as feeling is concerned, were few and far between for him. He wrote to Elizabeth Ritchie, "I am rarely led by impressions (i.e., spontaneous impulses), but generally by reason and by Scripture. I see abundantly more than I feel."

In his teachings he warned, however, against both undervaluing and overvaluing the place of reason in spiritual experience. He wrote:

> When therefore you depose or depreciate reason, you must not imagine you are doing God service. . .unless you willfully shut your eyes, you cannot but see of what service it is both in laying the foundation of true religion, under the guidance of the Spirit of God, and in raising the superstructure. . . .
>
> Permit me to add a few words to you, likewise, who overvalue reason. . . .Let reason do all that reason can: Employ it as far as it will go. But, at the same time, acknowledge it is utterly incapable of giving either faith, or hope, or love; and consequently, of producing either real virtue or substantial happiness.

On the other hand, in *A Plain Account of Christian Perfection* Wesley warned against over-dependence upon emotion in substantial religious experience. His second advice to those who would seek holiness and maintain the holy life contains these impassioned insights:

> Beware of that daughter of pride, *enthusiasm [today we would speak of fanaticism]!* Oh, keep at the utmost distance from it; give no place to a heated imagination. Do not hastily ascribe things to God. Do not easily suppose dreams, voices, impressions, visions, or revelations to be from God. They may be from him. They may be from nature. They may be from the devil. Therefore *believe not every spirit, but try the spirits whether they be of God.* Try all things by the written word, and let all bow down before it. You are in danger of enthusiasm every hour, if you depart ever so little from scripture;

yea, or from the plain literal meaning of any text, taken in connection with the context. And so you are, if you despise or lightly esteem reason, knowledge, or human learning, every one of which is an excellent gift of God, and may serve the noblest purposes.

I advise you, never to use the words *wisdom, reason,* or *knowledge* by way of reproach. On the contrary, pray that you yourself may abound in them more and more. If you mean *worldly* wisdom, *useless* knowledge, *false* reasoning, say so; and throw away the chaff, but not the wheat.

One general inlet to enthusiasm is expecting the end without the means; the expecting knowledge, for instance, without searching the scriptures, and consulting the children of God; the expecting spiritual strength without constant prayer, and steady watchfulness; the expecting any blessing without hearing the word of God at every opportunity.

In another place in the same work Wesley writes, "The very desire of growing in grace may sometimes be by an inlet of enthusiasm. As it continually leads us to seek new grace, it may lead us unawares to seek something else new, besides newer degrees of love to God and man." He strove for a wholesome balance between feeling and reason, insisting that "knowledge and vital piety must be joined."

That one of the functions of spiritual formation is to help effect such a balance between emotions and mind is illuminated by Robert C. Roberts in his volume *Spirituality and Human Emotion.*[10] Here is a summary of Roberts' progression of thought in this regard:

Whatever else Christianity may be, it is a set of emotions. It is love of God and neighbor, grief about one's own waywardness, joy in the merciful salvation of our God, gratitude, hope, and peace. . . . (p. 1)

Emotions are ways of "seeing" ourselves and our world that grow out of concerns of one sort or another. . . .The Christian emotions, then, are ways of "seeing" which are determined by the peculiar Christian concepts and the scheme of beliefs which give rise to those concepts. . . . (p. 11)

In the case of the Christian emotions, the terms of "seeing" ourselves and our world. . .grow out of concerns of one sort or another. . . . The Christian emotions, then, are ways of "seeing" which are determined by the peculiar Christian concepts and the scheme of beliefs which give rise to those concepts. . . . (p. 11)

In the case of the Christian emotions, the terms of "seeing" are provided by the Christian story. . . .It is important to Christians that emotions are partially within people's control, that they can be commanded. . . .Beliefs are dispositions, whereas emotions are occurrences in consciousness. . . .Belief is not enough for spirituality. Christians must not only believe, but also must learn to attend to the things of God. (pp. 23–24)

Roberts is pointing out not only the difference between beliefs and emotions but their necessary interrelationships. In the final analysis, our beliefs, our way of looking at life, our value judgments determine our concerns and these in turn are expressed in our emotions.

How important, then, spiritual formation is in relation to the control of both the mind and emotions of the growing Christian. Michael Green, Baptist theologian, author, preacher, evangelist, said recently, "It's tragic when you see evangelists producing classically bad theology. . . .But if evangelists need to become more scholarly, scholars also need to become more evangelistic. Once your mind is filled with the Lord, it ought to buzz out into every side of your life."[11]

Spiritual formation is growth in our love for God and others. We are to love God with both our minds and our hearts, and then we can better love our neighbors as ourselves.

Christians need an inner strength to face life's difficulties

Spiritual formation is imperative to provide an inner support system adequate for mastering the difficult circumstances of one's life. Some of these circumstances are inward—temptations, frustrations, stress, and the like. Other circumstances are outward—mere routine, failure, loss, overpowering work loads, and the expectations of others. Inevitably, inexplicable sufferings become our lot and press their heavy weight upon us.

Rufus Jones reminds us that

. . . what tends to unsettle us most is the dull daily friction, the slow wear and tear and attrition of life . . . the natural breakdown of things. The hardest thing to bear . . . is the stupid rolling on of the

dull insensible cartwheel, that blindly goes over and crushes without
any purpose what is most loved and dearest. "Ole man river, he
don't say nuthin'; he jes' keeps rollin' along."[12]

That circumstances can be overwhelming is a universal
experience. Medical doctors cite stress as a direct cause of at least
one-third of all sicknesses and claim that another third is indirectly
aggravated by stress. The late Dr. Hans Selye, who spent a
lifetime studying stress and who became the world's foremost
medical scholar on the subject, said that an individual at birth is
equipped with enough of what he calls "adaptation energy" to last
a lifetime. This pool of energy can only be depleted; it cannot be
replenished. It is very much like fueling a conventional airplane.
Once it takes off it cannot have its fuel replenished; it is expected
to carry enough fuel to last the entire trip with some reserve.
Under normal circumstances the adaptation energy that man is
given at birth should last his entire lifetime. However, this pool of
energy is drawn upon more heavily when the body is under stress,
and therefore may run out prematurely. In other words, stress
causes the living machinery to develop problems and to break
down sooner than it should. Those who are subject to a great deal
of stress risk having their effectiveness decreased and their
usefulness cut short.

Strictly speaking, it is not stress itself that hurts us but how
we react to stress. If we allow ourselves to react adversely, we
suffer the consequences. On the other hand, if we react to stress in
the right way, we can come off unhurt. It is like having good
shock absorbers on one's car.

Spiritual resources are shock absorbers that can protect one's
emotional and physical well-being from the bumps of stress. One
must capitalize on the power that comes through prayer. One
must take time to feed one's soul with the Word of God and the
literature of the saints. One must engage in those personal and
corporate disciplines which aid in the experience of wholeness. A
person must give one's self in service to others. All of this is
spiritual formation.

So inner personal resources prove to be the only adequate
support system in the midst of the temptations, legitimate
demands, trying situations, sufferings, and crises of one's life. The
writer of one of the *Letters of the Scattered Brotherhood* presents an

interesting insight. Writing about each person having both an *inner you* (one's true self) and an *outer you* (one's self enmeshed in life's circumstances), the author suggests that there are occasions when the inner you must withdraw from the outer you and say to the outer you, "I am stronger than you. I will enable you to master the circumstances."

For the inner you to remain stronger than the outer you, a continuous inward renewing and replenishing must take place. The body needs recreation. The mind must experience relaxation. Often the emotions need reconstitution. The spirit must have its times of refreshment. Always the will needs reinforcement.

Marten Ten Hoor writes, "Resources of the spirit are like savings: they must be accumulated before they are needed. When they are needed, there is no substitute for them. Sooner or later, the individual faces the world alone and that moment may overwhelm him if he has no resources within himself.

Spiritual replenishment is offered us through the process of spiritual formation. I quote again from the *Letters of the Scattered Brotherhood:*

> Call upon me in time of need and I will answer thee—is the most practical thing you can do. . . .Do not beseech for the Gift already given you. . . .Learn to receive, to accept and use it. (p. 135)
>
> These communions restore you because during the time of your quiet receiving from the source of the Spirit, you are bathed in the waters of life. This will keep you pure in heart and your bodies sweet with the Spirit; so illumined that you will not be fouled in the mire of human living. (p. 186)
>
> Therefore when effort is required of you in an endeavor which calls for high intelligence, give it to the Spirit within you to do, let him within you do the work as you were told, and you will pass among the heavy, selfish, material lives untouched and you will not be soiled and your body and your spirit will be protected and forever refreshed. You will not then have reactions, because the world will not have dominion over you (p. 186).[13]

When George Tyrell was having difficulties with the Jesuit Order, his spiritual director, Baron von Hugel, wrote him, reminding him that inner spiritual resources are the only adequacy for such crises in life.

Maxie Dunnam relates a delightful story told him by Bishop

Earl G. Hunt of the United Methodist Church. A friend of his, a traveling businessmen, frequently visited a great foundry, and he never missed the opportunity to study the workmen. One man, a furnace tender, was a veritable giant. It was a striking sight to watch him work—huge muscles rippling in unbroken rhythm, pools of perspiration glistening on his bare skin. He was rough, uncouth, a man of brawn. But once Hunt's friend saw the huge man stagger, almost overcome with the intense heat of the fires. He looked weary, ill, but he regained his footing, stepped away from the furnace, and passed a great blackened hand in gentle reverence over something hanging around his neck. It seemed to strengthen him, and in a moment he was back on the job. Curious, the friend peered more closely. He discovered that around the big workman's neck was a tiny crucifix suspended on a chain. It looked strange against its background, but it did something for that giant of a man. He could touch it and brush weariness aside. It was a fountain of refreshment and strength. He had found the secret.

I was Mildred Santosuosso's pastor for nearly nine years. I do not recall a person whose family had more continuing illness and trouble. For years she cared for her ailing parents, day after day, with no letup. There was also sickness within her immediate family. As a pastor, I probably was in her home more frequently than in any other in the parish. One day as I stood on the front porch bidding her good-bye after a pastoral visit, I asked, "Mildred, how do you stand it?" She immediately raised her hand and pointed upward and said, "I meet Him up there—in my bedroom."

Christians need to be engaged in redemptive ministries

Spiritual formation is imperative for a Christian to perform effectively the redemptive ministries assigned by Jesus Christ. In relation to ministry one must be sensitive to the mind of Christ, must be motivated by the love of Christ, must manifest the Spirit of Christ, and must experience the power of Christ.

Sensitivity to the mind of Christ enables one to discover what to do in the name of Christ. Such sensitivity is developed and heightened through the process of spiritual formation.

Motivation is indispensable in spiritual ministry. The only adequate motivation is the love of Christ. "The love of Christ compels me." Without the manifestation of the spirit of Christ, effective ministry is impossible. Ministry must be compassionate. Frank Laubach often speaks of love as the key to all witnessing to Christ. First Corinthians 13 will always be the most beautiful expression of the insistence upon love in spiritual experience. Frederick W. Faber exhorted Christians to love in ministry as he penned these poetic words: "And preach thee, too, as love knows how." Washington Gladden in his prayer-hymn bids us manifest compassion: "Help me the slow of heart to move / By some clear, winning word of love." Where else is love born apart from continuing spiritual devotion?

The power of Christ is also needed for ministry. Here again the secret is found in a personal relationship to Christ, sustained through the means of spiritual growth. "I can do all things through Christ which strengtheneth me" (Phil. 4:13, KJV). How often the apostle Paul speaks of Christ as the secret of power for ministry: "in Christ," "with Christ," "by Christ," "through Christ." C. S. Lewis reminds us that we must become ". . .as glass to let the white light without flame, the Father pass unstained."

Christians need a renewable inner strength so they can serve others

Spiritual formation is imperative to keep us replenished as we engage in ministries to others. Just as we need inner resources to master outward circumstances, so we need inner replenishment for continuing ministries. Ministry requires exertion, strength, stamina. In the process of ministry we understand something of what was said about Jesus, that He had often to withdraw to pray.

Frank Laubach speaks of the necessity of inner replenishment. He says that God must keep us full "if we are to give out to others. We cannot do more for the world than we really are. We cannot give what we do not have." At another time he writes, "As a spring of water must have more than we dip from it, so your soul must have much more than you give others." In the same vein, a Catholic sister from Thailand, studying in Manila, said to a friend of mine, "I find that that which I do not have I cannot give." Spiritual formation undergirds the normal rhythm of spiritual life and activity: life poured out, life renewed, life poured out, life renewed, and on and on.

Jan van Ruysbroeck (1293–1381) spoke of the rhythm of spiritual reality in these incisive words: "God is absolute repose and fecundity reconciled. . . .The Spirit of God breathes us out that we may love, and do good works; and draws us into Himself, that we may rest in fruition, and this is Eternal Life. . . .Action and fruition never hinder, but strengthen one another. . . .They are the double wings. . .that take us Home."

So spiritual formation makes possible a wholesome balance between the passive and active elements in personal spiritual experience. It takes the perspective of both Mary and Martha. Mary's sitting at the feet of Jesus should lead to serving. And Martha will serve better when she takes time to be quiet and become refreshed.

An analogy pictured in the *Letters of the Scattered Brotherhood* is intensely creative. Speaking of the results of times of spiritual refreshment, the author says, "You can carry well-filled water jars across 'no man's land' as you return to daily routine."

On a pleasure cruise one day, a nervous passenger paced up and down the deck watching the course of the boat as it sailed downriver. Unable to stand his worry any longer, he sought out the captain. "Captain," he asked, "are you sure you know where the rocks are?" "No, sir," the captain answered, "but I know where the channel is."

Once a person discovers the channel of God's ever-available adequacy through spiritual formation, the feared rocks of being over-burdened, exhausted beyond measure, or frustrated because of seeming failure assume their rightful proportions.

Christians need a proper balance between the material and the spiritual

Spiritual formation is imperative for the Christian to achieve a wholesome balance between the material and the spiritual. The material cannot be ignored or bypassed, but it must never become primary and take precedence over the spiritual. This is what Jesus was insisting upon as He spoke to the people after the feeding of the five thousand:

You are looking for me because you ate the bread and had all you wanted, not because you saw my works of power. Do not work for food that spoils; instead work for the food that lasts for eternal life. This food the Son of Man will give you. . .I am the bread of life. He who comes to me will never be hungry; he who believes in me will never be thirsty (John 6:26–27, 35, TEV).

The world is too much with us. The 1983 report of the Lausanne Committee on World Evangelization declares, "The Westernizing and modernizing trends of the world are rapidly moving Christians away from commitment to prayer and meditation upon the person of Christ." There is constant tension between the worldly and the spiritual.

> Who is master? the world or you?
> It is the eternal struggle:
> the world, so dramatic, so exciting;
> the Spirit, so gentle, so. . .still.[14]

Yielding to the world is spiritually fatal. Robert Bellah says this in unmistakable words: "The price of neglect of the interior life is the reification of the superficial, an entrapment in the world of existing objects and structures." Victory over the world can be won only through spiritual formation. To wash away the heavy oiliness of materialism is a task requiring constant vigilance and discipline.

Jesus always kept the primary focus upon spirituality in the midst of the tensions with materiality. He calls upon Christians to do the same. Commenting upon Matthew 6:19–21, John Wesley wrote, "I lay up no treasures upon earth: I lay up nothing at all. I cannot help leaving my book [assets] behind me whenever God calls me home; but, in every other respect, my own hands will be my executors."

Without doubt the seed of such concern for the precedence of spirituality over the world was implanted in Wesley's mind and heart early in life in the Epworth rectory. His mother, Susanna, who was his teacher and spiritual guide, wrote in her devotional journal:

> Were I permitted to choose a state of life, or positively to ask of God anything in this world, I would humbly choose and beg that I might be placed in such a Station, wherein I might have daily bread with moderate care without so much hurry and distraction; and that

I might have more leisure to retire from the world, without injuring my [?husband] or Children.[15]

Christians need a balance between a focus on themselves and a focus on the common life

Spiritual formation is imperative as an antidote to excessive individualism in spiritual experience. Even though certain aspects of spiritual formation are intensely personal, some processes in spiritual growth are best carried on in active relationship with others. The pursuit of personal spiritual growth must never be viewed as a process isolated from our common human life or from the life of the community of faith of which we are a part. Every individual's life is bound up with the destiny of the total community. So in a very real sense, spiritual formation is always corporate as well as personal.

This active relationship with others in spiritual formation is particularly manifest in that vehicle for spiritual growth known as spiritual direction. John Henry Newman speaks of taking the spiritual advice of others as God's way. Baron Friedrich von Hugel wrote, "Behind every saint stands another saint. That is the great tradition. I never learnt anything myself by my own old nose."[16] Thomas Merton concluded that "in all contemplative traditions, it has been found necessary that those who have attained to some depth of religious insight should to some extent guide others who seek to attain the same experience of truth in their own lives."[17]

Christians need to recover a sense of the personal in their faith and guard it against the blights of institutionalism and rationalism

Spiritual formation is imperative to withstand the blights of institutionalism and rationalism. The Reformation was a needed rediscovery of the personal in religion, but such a rediscovery had to be sustained by a constant emphasis upon the personal because of the inroads of institutionalism.

The rise of such a significant body of devotional literature in seventeenth- and eighteenth-century England was a necessary safeguard against the institutionalization of the doctrine of justification by faith. Nominal churchmanship or mere adherence to moral codes are never adequate stimuli to spiritual growth.[18]

There is always the danger of rationalism creeping into our religious thinking. It dilutes the content of every evangelical doctrine and has to be countered persistently, as someone said, by "a renewed sense of wonder and by a vivid realization of God's personal work among people." A few years ago a Christian thinker regained an evangelical doctrine of Christ. He said, "My high Christology grew out of a developing personal inwardness." Thus, spiritual formation had been instrumental in revitalizing his theology.

What more adequate summary statement could be made of the imperatives of spiritual formation than this: "The search for sainthood is the secret of growth and stability of the Christian community."

We have considered eleven reasons for spiritual formation. We could say much more about each one, but I hope enough has been said to convince you that spiritual formation is imperative for the Christian and to compel you to engage in it both personally and corporately.

C. S. Lewis is insistent upon the necessity of spiritual growth in the Christian's life. We close this chapter with some of his convictions about spiritual formation which are quoted by Leanne Payne in her book, *Real Presence:*[19]

> One's conversion does not guarantee that a soul will continue to progress in its imitation of Christ. There is always the matter of (1) resisting temptation and (2) struggling against the pride and spiritual ignorance of one's heart. (pp. 71–72, 76)
> One dies to the old self and lives to the new by continuing to receive of that other life. (p. 77)
> Christianity isn't a covenant or a law but it is a life—it is Another Life being lived in and through us. (p. 78)
> You do not fail in obedience through lack of love, but have lost love because you never attempted obedience. (p. 81)
> It is possible once we have begun on the road to sanctity and humility to forget whence we have come. (p. 76)
> It is only by remembering that "Another lives in me" that we can die daily to that old false, usurping self, and that we continue to be drawn "farther in and higher up" into the life of God. (p. 77)
> A Christian can lose the Christ-life which has been put into him, and he has to make efforts to keep it. (p. 98)

So we have the paradox: In one sense, the road back to God is a road of moral effort, of trying harder and harder. But in another sense it is not trying that is ever going to bring us home. All this leads up to the vital moment at which you turn to God and say, "You must do this. I can't." (p. 99)

NOTES

[1] Mary Strong, ed., *Letters of the Scattered Brotherhood* (New York: Harper, 1948), 92.

[2] Miriam Murphy, *Prayer in Action* (Nashville: Abingdon, 1979).

[3] Bryant, *Wesley Reader*, 213.

[4] Friedrich von Hugel, *Spiritual Counsel and Letters of Baron Friedrich von Hugel*, ed. Douglas V. Steere (New York: Harper, 1964), 46.

[5] Ibid., 90–91.

[6] Bryant, *Wesley Reader*, 241–42.

[7] Richard Schickel, "Sellers Strikes Again," *Time* (March 3, 1980): 64ff.

[8] Ardis Whitman, "The Awesome Power to Be Ourselves," *The Reader's Digest* (January 1983): 79–82.

[9] Von Hugel, *Spiritual Counsel*, 95.

[10] Robert C. Roberts, *Spirituality and Human Emotion* (Grand Rapids: Eerdmans, 1982).

[11] Michael Green, "Gleanings: Scholarly Evangelism: No Apologies," *Evangelical Newsletter* 11, no. 10 (May 11, 1984): 2.

[12] Rufus M. Jones, *The Radiant Life* (New York: Macmillan, 1944), 8.

[13] Strong, *Scattered Brotherhood*, 91.

[14] Ibid., 94.

[15] Cited by Charles Wallace, Jr., "Susanna Wesley's Spirituality: The Freedom of a Christian Woman," *Methodist History* 22, no. 3 (April 1984): 158.

[16] Friedrich von Hugel, *Essays and Addresses on the Philosophy of Religion* (New York: Dutton, 1921).

[17] Thomas Merton, *Contemplation in a World of Action* (Garden City, N. Y.: Doubleday, 1971).

[18] Cf. Stranks, *Anglican Devotion*.

[19] Leanne Payne, *Real Presence: The Holy Spirit in the Works of C. S. Lewis* (Westchester, Ill.: Cornerstone, 1979).

5

THREE ESSENTIAL CHARACTERISTICS

There are three essential characteristics of any plan of spiritual formation, whether it be personal or corporate. Spiritual formation must be intentional, structured, and disciplined.

INTENTIONAL

Spiritual life, like all life, is never static; it either progresses or regresses. There is either developing, unfolding life or death. The Christian ideal is to grow in and into Christlikeness. But spiritual growth is never automatic; it does not just happen. We have to make it happen. While it is true that God takes the initiative in offering us the possibility of spiritual growth, we must respond by participating in the process to make it happen. The Christian life engages our emotions and our minds, but it also requires our wills. This is especially true when it comes to spiritual formation. Before we can grow spiritually we must first *want* to grow.

A Buddhist story tells of someone coming to a spiritual master, asking for the way to enlightenment. The master took him to a lake and held his head under water for a long time. When he finally let the aspirant up, gasping for breath, the master told him, "You must want enlightenment as much as you just wanted air to live."[1]

In St. Benedict's sixth-century *Rule for Monks,* he says of those who knock at the monastery door:

> When anyone is newly come from the reformation of his life, let him not be granted an easy entrance. [Instead, if the newcomer] perseveres in his knocking and if it is seen after four or five days that he bears patiently the harsh treatment offered him and the difficulty of admission, and that he persists in his petition, then let entrance be granted to him.[2]

Spiritual formation calls for divine-human cooperation, and before we can grow spiritually, we must recognize that. While God is working in us, we are also working out our own salvation with fear and trembling. Some things God will not do for us. He will not search the Scriptures for us. He will not make us pray. He will not make us resist evil. He will not make us assume essential spiritual disciplines. The Christian life is more than a superficial acquiescence to the teachings of Jesus and an unrealistic reliance upon divine power. It must involve a Person indwelling us so that in cooperation with Him we are enabled to experience both His will and good pleasure.

Such biblical imperatives as "fight the good fight of faith," "stand fast," "pray without ceasing," "be strong," "lay hold of eternal life," "examine yourselves," "be vigilant," "grow in the grace and the knowledge of the Lord Jesus Christ" are evidence of our personal responsibility in the process of spiritual growth. God will not do for us what He expects us to do for ourselves.

Paul summarizes it when he writes in Colossians 1:22–23 (RSV) that Christ desires "to present you holy and blameless and irreproachable before him provided that you continue. . . ."

Our response to God's grace makes possible the further gift of God's graces. Grace is always sufficient, provided we are ready to cooperate with it. Graces are the free gifts God bestows on each of us as a result of our response to His grace. They help us grow more Christlike and bring us closer to achieving His will for us. I once jotted the following notes as Frank Laubach spoke of this divine-human cooperative process in spiritual development:

> Our part—to believe and to let His aching tenderness flood our lives, fill us to overflowing. We will change the world by spilling over with Christ.
>
> My light shines only when the switch is on. Help me not to flicker today.

God is flowing water. We must keep the well open. God is electric current. We must keep good connections. God is gasoline. We must keep the lines open from the tank to the engine.

When we speak of intention we mean putting the full weight of one's will on the side of spiritual formation. All the saints through the ages agree on the importance of total dedication and determination.

Johannes Tauler (1300–1361) wrote, "He has all power in heaven and earth, but the power to do His work in man against man's will, He has not got."

St. Catherine of Genoa (1447–1510) spoke of "the soul's self-chosen intrinsic purification."

Baron Friedrich von Hugel (1852–1925) had much to say about the indispensable place of the will in spiritual nurture:

> You and I will, in a most real sense, be tomorrow different, fuller or lesser, and truer or falser, personalities than we are today, and this not simply automatically, but entirely through the more or less deliberate acts and acceptances of our volitional nature, and the countless effects and habits of its past volitional history as thus now again endorsed or revoked, and the grace of God working in and through these our acts will take place within the next twenty-four hours.

> . . . a very rich, deep, true, straight and simple growth in the love of God, accepted and willed gently but greatly, at the daily, hourly cost of self.[3]

Frank Laubach emphasized "will-pressure," "will-bent," "will-act" as one's responsibility for spiritual growth. His actual words are illustrative:

> God can reach us only when we will attention to Him.

> God, help me to continue gentle but incessant pressure on the will—on and on and on!

> God, this attempt to keep my *will* bent toward thy will is integrating me. . . . My task is a simple one after all. It is just to guard this will. Religion comes to us today to be not doctrine or faith primarily, but rather the directed will. That is my task—to hold my will close to the current power, and let thee sweep through endlessly.

> "WILL ACT" is my responsibility. The rest God will attend to.

> Push your will all day, all this hour in His direction, saying, I am trying to do thy will. . . .

> It is simple now; my will must be pressed toward thee, endlessly and gently toward thee.

> Living on the highest plane is a matter of constant choice of the highest thing to think, or see, or do at each moment. (Notes from a Laubach lecture)

The *Letters of the Scattered Brotherhood* covers the whole gamut of spiritual experience. They, too, insist upon the importance of the will. One's will is spoken of as "law in that small commonwealth" (of one's inner life) (p. 12). The reader is reminded that "the will to win is an important part of the spiritual armor" (p. 40) and consequently is exhorted to "keep a naked intent toward God" (pp. 33, 46, 85, 87, 107, 115). Personal determination in the direction of the spiritual life—"I make up my mind," "I will" (pp. 7–8), is a constant refrain of all the letters in the volume.

Intention in the direction of spiritual formation grows out of intense spiritual desire. Frederick W. Faber commented that "the lack of desire is the ill of all ills." A holy man once remarked, "At any given moment you are just as holy as you want to be." Such intense spiritual desire for spiritual growth is the result of a deep sense of personal need. The stimulus to Christian growth is a personal awareness of its impossibility apart from resources outside one's self.

The saints of the ages, who have made spiritual growth a priority in their lives, have expressed in unmistakable terms their deep sense of inner need. Oswald Chambers wrote:

> What a joyous life the life hid with Christ in God is! But, my God, I dare not for one moment think how far short of it I fall in spite of all thy grace and patience. But thou art making me, and I thank thee.

> . . . my spirit longs that thy energizing life may flow in and through me more, and still yet more. But how unbeautiful I am, how un-Christianlike, and yet it is not in depression, but in amazing hope I see this.

In my present mood I am inclined to give way to the feeling of having missed the mark.

One is amazed at the repeated confessions of Frank Laubach about what he considers his spiritual "failures" and by his desperate pleas for God's grace to help him improve himself spiritually. An entire chapter could be devoted to the experiences and writings of Laubach in this regard, but only a few of his statements must suffice:

Overwhelmed by the sense of thy stupendously immense power and size and wisdom . . . and of my own stupid, blundering, frail little soul and body, I am ashamed. . . .

How far—how far we are from that objective! What worms compared to the sons we are yet to become.

Pure as thou art and impure as I have been. . . .

Frustrated in most of my life efforts by a mediocrity which sends others ahead. . . .

Looking back over all the years that have gone, I see my life filled with glorious opportunities—lost. And the reason is very plain. I was too far from thee, God, to meet those opportunities. . . . It is a doleful, heart-sickening sense of remorse. . . .

My conscience troubles me; too many situations have defeated me. I am afraid of people. . . . High above me there appear the Himalayas of character that show how far down I still am.

God, very humble and sensible of the feebleness of my service, I hate myself this grey dawn. It would be easy to lapse into morbid self-pity.

. . . the wide chasm between ourselves and thee. There is so much—and the longer one looks at thee the more one hates himself—that it leaves one self-condemned and wondering at thy forgiveness. Why shouldest thou care at all for this ugly me? (Personal notes)

Laubach sensed constantly his need for spiritual growth. He was keenly aware of his total dependence upon the grace of God to make it possible. But he never shirked his responsibility to cooperate fully with the processes of divine grace.

Those Himalayas of the spirit life help me realize what a mean, low thing I am . . . but we can rise! God, let us get our teeth into this day and see what we can do with it. . . . Just a day full of "Yes, Lord, yes."

We have so much, much more than we suspect to be burned out of our souls, and fire must be used. Sweetness alone will not finish the work, nor even begin to touch the deep vice and selfishness that spoil the soul. Then, God, work thy purifying, for I know I need it . . . (but not how much I need it). (Personal notes)

In a dialogue with God, Laubach asks, "But what of my ugly sins, Lord?" God answers, "I will burn, burn, burn them out until you are wholly pure." (Personal notes)

W. E. Sangster closes his book, *The Secret of Radiant Life,*[4] with the following stanzas which express the Christian's continuing sense of need during his entire spiritual pilgrimage.

> Lord Jesus, I am longing
> From sin to be set free;
> To find my deep desiring
> Forever fixed on Thee.
> All hope I now abandon
> Myself to conquer sin;
> Invade my willing nature
> And come and dwell within.
>
> The passing years oppress me,
> My growth in grace so slow;
> My wayward, fickle cravings
> Have leagued me to the foe;
> Myself to self disloyal,
> I loathe, yet love my sin;
> Now hear my heartfelt pleading
> And come and dwell within.
>
> If Thou shoulds't stand close by me
> 'Tis more than I deserve;
> But, being still outside me,
> From virtue yet I swerve.
> Come nearer, Lord, than near me,
> My succor to begin
> Usurp the heart that craves Thee!
> O come and dwell within.

Intentionality to spiritual formation means keeping one's total self fully open and receptive to God's Spirit continually. This calls for developing constant sensitivity, receptivity, and obedience. There must be the continuing personal intention of one's will—the exercise of continuing choices in the direction of spiritual formation. This means practicing the presence of God.

Laubach is our mentor in every aspect of spiritual experience. He writes that the heart of religion and even of life is to practice the constant presence of God. He reminds himself, and all Christians, that the important matter is "how to live each minute of the day for Christ—how to let Christ have complete control of one's thoughts all day—so that they shall grow in one's mind like lovely flowers planted by God."

Laubach prays, "Every minute, Christ, every minute aware of thee!" (Personal notes)

E. Stanley Jones, in his own inimitable way, summarizes the Christian's constant need of total receptivity and obedience:

One thing I know—the MIND—to know Christ;
One thing have I desired—the EMOTIONS—to love Christ;
One thing I do—the WILL—to obey Christ."[5]

At one point in the play, *Hay Fever,* the leading actress says to a gentleman, "Come and lean attentively on the piano." The instructions were freighted with meaning: "Don't be just a casual observer of my piano playing; be attentive to my piano playing." If we are to grow spiritually, we dare not be mere observers of sacred things. We must give wholehearted attention to all those things that contribute to spiritual formation. Such attention grows out of intention.

STRUCTURED

Spiritual formation also needs to be structured. It is the testimony of personal experience that unless spiritual formation is structured it is not carried on effectively. In *Letters of the Scattered Brotherhood* the reader is reminded, "Many of your defenses are down, not through bodily discomforts, but through an unordered rhythm. To some this idea of ORDER irritates the mind, but that is a false suggestion from your Outer You; for order, alertness, awareness of the divine companion is rest" (p. 101).

Rufus J. Womble, American Episcopal clergyman writes, "We cannot ooze into the Kingdom of God or into growing spiritually. But we enter the Kingdom and grow spiritually by definite, concrete actual decisions by letting God's Holy Spirit make one change in us after another."

Spiritual formation cannot be pursued haphazardly. In one's adventure toward growth the Christian must take an active part in one's own development by discovering and following a working method by which one can live as a channel for the Holy Spirit to flow into one's life for one's wholeness and through one's life for the healing of others.

In seeking to discover a structured plan for spiritual formation, both personally and corporately, one must keep in mind the necessity of a wholesome balance between the interior life and outward activity. Evelyn Underhill, contemporary mystic, achieved such a balance. She spent the mornings researching and writing her volume on mysticism. She socialized in the afternoons. Her spiritual director, Baron Friedrich von Hugel, suggested that she visit the poor two afternoons a week.

Evelyn Underhill wrote to a new "spiritual adventurer":

> Develop and expand the wholesome, natural, and intellectual interests in your life . . . don't allow yourself to concentrate on the religious side only. Remember ALL life comes to you from God, and is to be used for Him . . . So live it all, and get the necessary variety and refreshment without which religious intensity soon becomes stale. . . .[6]

Rufus Jones, another mystical leader of this century, believed that the "great life" is a noble fusion of serenity and adventure. He said we always fight better after "the pause."[7]

Ernest Boyer, writing in *Sojourners* magazine (July–August 1983), speaks of balancing the spiritualities of solitude and community. Longing and caring are two ways to seek the divine. They are like two parts of a wheel. Longing is the edge of the wheel. The life it offers is one of exhilaration and speed, but at times also grinding. Caring is the wheel's center. Slower and duller, it is also close to the core of things.

The spirituality of life on the edge is an answer to the longing from transformation, the hunger for the presence of God, a craving for the transcendent. The spirituality of community is one that answers the human need to love and care for others.

The necessary balance between devotion and action is seen vividly in the development of a healthy prayer life. Martin

Thornton insists that prayer must be learned and practiced "when things are going well"; "even before the crisis."

> . . . seek direction in prayer when things are going well; when you are cool, calm, and collected—or rather recollected. Prayer is a positive adventure, not a negative duty. . . . All parish priests have seen the frustration and fear in those who suddenly seek consolation from prayer and religion in bereavement; the callous but true answer is that they should have got down to the matter twelve months earlier. If you are on a sinking ship in the middle of the ocean, it is a bit late to learn to swim. Look on the prayer in terms of adventure and proficiency at least as well as devotion. Do not wait for disaster.[8]

A structured plan of spiritual formation must be developed within clearly defined parameters and undergirded by a sound biblical theology and be Christ-centered in its focus. It must be people-oriented, always in the direction of love. As Frank Laubach said, "The expression of love to others is a dominant note in all spiritual formation." And he was constantly seeking such love: "Help, God, that today I may take the whole roof off my soul and let thee pack every corner with love every minute of today."

Also, a structured plan of spiritual formation must be personally congenial. By this I mean, adjusted to one's present spiritual state, and possible of fulfillment in view of one's daily circumstances. Certainly not everybody is expected to pursue spiritual growth along the same avenues, always utilizing the same techniques, particularly those which are stereotyped.

Of course, every spiritual pilgrim should study the Bible. But not every person will begin with the deep mystical insights of the gospel according to John when the basic truths about the life and ministry of Jesus as recorded in the synoptics are yet to be learned.

In developing one's prayer life the beginner will not start with meditation and contemplation. In reference to personal disciplines, it would be spiritually fatal to try to handle all the needed disciplines at once. The needs for personal discipline must be listed according to priority, and the greatest need must be dealt with first.

Not everyone can afford the luxury of an hour of solitude and devotion before going to work in the morning. But it will have to be determined what the Christian who wants to grow will do with the fifteen or so minutes at one's disposal, and how other periods in the day can be utilized for devotion. Certainly not everybody will find it congenial to keep a prayer-journal.

A structured plan of spiritual formation will, of necessity, include the use of the divinely-appointed means of grace, including corporate worship and participation in the Lord's Supper, and the practice of both personal and corporate spiritual disciplines. But the exact way in which the means of grace are utilized and the disciplines practiced will need to be worked into a plan which is as congenial as possible for the person who expects to benefit by it.

In the next section of this book, as we discuss the Centenary Model, we will deal specifically with ten areas deemed essential for spiritual growth and how a structured plan relates to each area.

DISCIPLINED

Spiritual formation is intentional. It is structured. It must also be disciplined. Thomas Merton wrote, "It is not complicated to lead the spiritual life but it is difficult"[9]

When I use the term *disciplined,* I am not referring primarily to the practice of spiritual disciplines, either personal or corporate, which is a necessary part of spiritual growth. Rather, I am thinking of the spirit and manner with which a person participates in the process of spiritual formation.

Discipline means totality of dedication. One's intention to achieve spiritual growth remains constant and such constancy is deepened continually. Dedication has both positive and negative elements. On the positive side, it involves the handing over of one's self totally to those things which contribute to spiritual growth.

On the negative side, dedication includes the determination to avoid the things that hinder spiritual growth. Henry J. Baron, professor of English at Calvin College, expressed his concern about the negative influences of television upon the spirituality of individuals and the church. He writes, "Television promotes a spirit of passivity; it tends to bypass our critical faculty and by neglect diminish it." He goes on to say that the commitment which the media desire is often in direct opposition to commitment to the will of God through Jesus Christ. "Television ushers into our homes a variety of hucksters and entertainers who by sheer repetition and beguiling charm effectively persuade the passive, captivated viewers of a set of values that are antithetical to a Christian confession and commitment."[10]

Disciplined means regularity and continuity in one's devotion and practice of the disciplines required for spiritual growth. John Wesley said that he intended to keep his prayer time early each morning "without exception." Oswald Chambers said it well: "You no more need a holiday from spiritual concentration than your heart needs a holiday from beating. You cannot have a moral holiday and remain moral, nor can you have a spiritual holiday and remain spiritual."[11]

Continuity and regularity are necessary in spite of one's feelings and moods. William James advised, "I think we ought to be independent of our moods, look on them as external (for they come to us unbidden), and feel if possible neither elated or depressed, but keep our eyes upon our work. . . ." This counsel reminds me of a remark by a mature Christian whom I heard when I was a college student: "I have learned to feel as good when I don't feel good as I feel when I do feel good."

Dietrich Bonhoeffer in his writings on the Christian life, particularly in *Life Together*, deals with the matter of moods and faith. He concludes emphatically that we must arrive at that state when our spirituality is never subject to our moods.

Martin Thornton, Anglican priest and professor of theology in this century, in *Christian Proficiency*, comments:

> Emotion plays a good, rightful, and important part in religious life. Private prayer without any feeling at all would be unbearable for most of us, but emotion and feeling must be disciplined and understood. . . . The one vital point for us is simply this: it cannot be said too often that the only certain guide to spiritual progress is moral theology—we are making progress in prayer when we commit fewer sins.[12]

Talking about Christians who took spiritual growth seriously, John Wesley wrote, "They strove, they agonized without intermission, to enter in at the straight gate. . . . They spared no pains to arrive at the summit of Christian holiness."

Disciplined means persistence. Spiritual growth is not achieved in ten easy lessons. It does not happen overnight (nor does one of God's beautiful redwood trees grow overnight). Frank Laubach says, "It is a long process. Souls take longer than diamonds to form." Spiritual formation takes time. We must give the Holy Spirit time to move upon us and within us. As the devotional hymn suggests, we must "take time to be holy."

Because spiritual formation is a process always demanding and sometimes almost overwhelming, there is the human tendency to become discouraged, particularly when a person does not seem to see much progress. But every form of therapy, whether physical or psychological or spiritual, to be effective demands persistence. Jesus reminded His followers to pray and never to faint. After we have put our hands to the plow we are not to look back. It may not be enough merely to "ask"—or even to "seek"— we must also "knock." The writings of the early apostles and our fathers and mothers in the faith across the centuries continually exhort the Christian to "keep the faith," "continue in the faith," "be faithful," "persevere to the end."

We need to remember that not only seeming failure, but also a little success can sometimes interrupt the pattern of persistence. I chuckle every time I remember my father telling me that he stopped his piano lessons after he learned to play "America."

John Bunyan (1628–1688) was exemplary in his life of disciplined perseverance. He wrote: "I have resolved . . . to run when I can, to go when I cannot run, and to creep where I cannot go. As to the main, I thank Him who loves me, I am fixed; my way is before me, my mind is beyond the River that has no bridge."[13]

Disciplined involves occasions of serious self-examination. Every vital organism, personal or institutional, must be willing to face itself realistically, honestly, evaluatively. I have just come from a meeting of the Rotary Club. Today was the transition meeting between the old Rotary year and the new one. The retiring president spoke incisively of the need of the club on such a significant occasion to do some serious evaluation of what has and has not been done during the past year and of what needs to be done in the year just ahead. Just so, in the process of spiritual formation there must be times when we take stock. A word of warning is in order, however. We can overdo this matter of introspection to our own undoing.

This can be illustrated from the early devotional life of John

Wesley. Dr. Steve Harper tells about this in an article entitled, "Wesley's Devotional Tips for Late Risers":

> Around 1732 his devotional life took a turn toward extreme self-examination. He became preoccupied with taking his spiritual pulse. At the back of his personal diary (not to be confused with his published journal), he devised an elaborate system by which he checked his spiritual progress, or lack of it. He even had a special symbol in the daily entries of his diary by which we could evaluate the fervency of his prayers! By his own admission, this extreme introspection threw his devotional life out of balance. By almost continually focusing on his faults, Wesley was practicing "defeatist devotionalism."[14]

So Wesley discovered that unless one is careful there is a subtle tendency to slip into a devotional pattern that accentuates the negative. Therefore, he proceeded to focus not primarily upon problems, but upon God's grace to meet those problems.

If carried on in a positive manner, and with the proper objectives in mind, self-evaluation can be conducted in a way that is totally beneficial to the one who would experience spiritual growth. Many plans of self-evaluation have been suggested, some of them more severe than others. For illustration, Susanna Wesley, in her devotional journal, suggested the practice of self-examination several times each day:

> Keep the mind in a temper for recollection, and often in the day call it in from outward objects, lest it wander into forbidden paths. Make an Examin(ation) of your Cons(cience) at least 3 times a day, and omit no opportunity of retirement from the world.[15]

John Fletcher, Anglican vicar of Madeley, England, one of the early theological leaders in the Wesleyan revival, a close friend of John Wesley, asked himself every night these questions:

> Did I awake spiritual and was I watchful in keeping my mind from wandering this morning?

> Have I this day got nearer to God in prayer or have I given way to a lazy, idle spirit?

> Has my faith been weakened by unwatchfulness or quickened by diligence?

> Have I walked by faith and seen God in all things?

Have I made the most of my time as far as I had light, strength and opportunity?

Have I denied myself in all unkind words and thoughts? Have I been delighted at seeing others preferred?

What have I done this day for the souls and bodies of God's dear saints?

Have I laid out anything to please myself, when I might have saved the money for the cause of God?

Do my life and conversation adorn the gospel of Jesus Christ?

Have I governed my tongue well this day, remembering that "in the multitude of words there wanteth not sin?"[16]

Others have used a once-a-week spiritual checkup. Some suggest a more detailed self-evaluation at less frequent intervals. One of the frequent recommendations now seems to be for the individual dedicated to spiritual formation to go on a quarterly retreat, alone, at least for a day, and dare to face oneself honestly, under the illumination of the Spirit of God.

Numerous evaluative instruments have been devised for such periodic self-examination. The beginner in spiritual formation may want to use an instrument already designed. There follows a sample of such an instrument based on W. E. Sangster's pamphlet, *A Spiritual Check-up.*

IN THE WORLD

Do I speak the truth?
Am I a person of the strictest honesty?
Do I pay my debts?
Do I fake my income tax returns?
Do I swear?
Do I tell suggestive stories?
In my relations with the other sex, am I pure in deed? word? thought?

O God, it is strange how low one can fall who professes to walk in Thy ways, and how separate one can keep the different parts of his life.

I would be one person: Thy person. Help me, for Jesus Christ's sake, Amen.

WHERE I WORK

Am I known as a Christian where I work?

Is Christ loved more at my place of business because of the way I live?

Are some people outside the Church because I am inside?

If I have concealed my discipleship, is it because I am afraid that my life would not sustain my profession? would not show I am ashamed of Christ? would show I am just a coward?

If I am ashamed of Christ, should it seem surprising if, at the Great Judgment, He is ashamed of me?

Ashamed of Jesus? Sooner far
Let evening blush to own a star . . .
And O may this my glory be
That Christ is not ashamed of me!

IN THE HOME

Do those who know me best believe in me most?

In the morning, half-awake, and in the evening, over-tired, am I still a Christian, courteous, grateful, good-humored?

Do I acknowledge God (guests or no guests) with grace before meals; and do I ever call the family to prayer? Gracious Father, I am ashamed to be guilty of discourtesy at home which would be unthinkable elsewhere, and that where I am loved most, I sometimes act worst. I mean to end all that. Help me, for Christ's sake, Amen.

IN MY HEART

Am I converted?

Have I given myself to God without any reserve?

Do I live day by day in conscious dependence on Him, and am I alert to the guidance of Heaven?

Do I find time every day for Bible study? unhurried prayer? quiet listening to God?

Do I love God's Day? His Word? His Holy Table?

Do I seek fellowship with other Christians in the week? O God, Teach me to love Thy Word, Thy House, Thy Table, and (through them all) Thyself. For the Saviour's sake, Amen.

WITH MY POSSESSIONS

How much money do I give to God?

Let it be granted that a Christian may spend part of his money on pleasure; ought I not to give at least as much to God as I spend on my own enjoyment? But have I?

Let me add it up honestly. Tobacco, movies, the theater, sport, personal adornment, joy-rides, this . . . and that . . . ? God forgive me!—I have been mean with God.

What about tithing?

Everything precious He gave me. I have given Him . . . ?

Bountiful God, if what we give thee is stored for us in Heaven, how well-off in Heaven will I be? I guess and fear. Forgive my meanness, for Christ's sake, Amen.

However, as one matures in the spiritual life one may want to design one's own evaluative instrument. As a result of serious self-examination one is aided in setting priorities according to one's devotional and disciplinary needs and in deciding when to expand into other areas of spiritual devotion and discipline and ministry.

This matter of examination and evaluation is just as relevant for corporate plans of spiritual formation. Small groups in particular, and churches that have corporate plans of spiritual formation must be just as concerned about regular times of evaluation.

When we discuss the Centenary Model in the next section of this book, I will mention actual evaluative surveys taken during the implementation of the corporate plan of spiritual formation in that congregation.

NOTES

[1] Tilden Edwards, *Living Simply Through the Day* (New York: Paulist, 1977), 222.

[2] Ibid., 59.

[3] Von Hugel, *Spiritual Counsel*, 47, 83.

[4] William E. Sangster, *The Secret of Radiant Life* (Nashville: Abingdon, 1957), 219.

[5] E. Stanley Jones, *Growing Spiritually* (Nashville: Abingdon, 1953), 338.

[6] Evelyn Underhill, *The Letters of Evelyn Underhill* (London: Religious Book Club, 1945), 175.

[7] R. Jones, *The Radiant Life*, 10–11.

[8] Neufelder and Coelho, *Spiritual Direction*, 55.

[9] Thomas Merton, *The Sign of Jonas* (London: Hollis and Carter, 1953).

[10] Henry J. Baron, "Gleanings: A Reminder for All Christians: TV May be Stunting Your Growth," *Evangelical Newsletter* 11 (May 25, 1984): 2.

[11] Oswald Chambers, *My Utmost for His Highest* (London: Simpkin Marshall, 1936), 106.

[12] Martin Thornton, *Christian Proficiency* (London: S.P.C.K., 1959), 28.

[13] Strong, *Scattered Brotherhood*, 134.

[14] Steve Harper, "Wesley's Devotional Tips for Late Risers," *Asbury Theological Seminary Herald* 93, no. 2 (March/April 1981): 9.

[15] Wallace, "Susanna Wesley," 161.

[16] Luke Tyerman, *Wesley's Designated Successor: The Life, Letters, and Literary Labours of the Rev. John William Fletcher* (London: Hodder and Stoughton, 1882).

6

THE CENTENARY MODEL
HOW IT WAS CREATED

Against the background of the discussion of the nature and imperatives of spiritual formation, and the supportive testimony to its validity from both the Bible and the Wesleyan way, we move now to discussion of a particular model of a church-wide plan of spiritual formation: The Centenary Model. The roots of Centenary Church go back 118 years. However, the present Centenary has experienced its rapid growth and expanding influence during the last three decades. Centenary is evangelical in theology, evangelistic in outreach, and unusually social-minded. The present membership has reached 2,500.

As stated in the Introduction, I joined the Centenary staff as a part-time member, with the express purpose of creating and directing a church-wide program of spiritual formation. I approached my task with certain basic convictions. First, Centenary Church, like every local church I know, needed a structured plan of spiritual formation for the entire congregation. Second, any plan of spiritual formation to be effective in an active, progressive church like Centenary would have to be developed from within the officiary and membership of the church rather than presented from the outside. In other words, I knew that if I tried to hand them a plan which I had already developed and insisted upon its adoption, it would never work. Third, I knew it would not be easy to incorporate such a plan of spiritual formation into a church that was already well-organized and with a crowded program of activities. I was aware of the challenge, both spiritual and administrative, that faced me.

OWNERSHIP

From the beginning, I insisted that the ownership of the plan of spiritual formation belong to the local church. I asked the senior minister to select a planning committee with which I could work during the development of the plan. This planning committee was intended to be truly representative of the several publics in the church who were deeply concerned about spiritual life and activity.

Forty persons were invited to serve on the original planning committee. Among these were representatives of the ministerial staff, the chairpersons of the various work areas, and representatives of the different age groups. A nucleus of the group was comprised of individual members who had been giving continuous evidence of their concern about spirituality. Included in the letter of invitation to prospective members of the planning committee were suggested dates for meetings during a six-month period.

In order to have pertinent data for the planning committee when it began its meetings, a survey relating to spiritual life was taken at the two church services on a designated Sunday morning. It is significant that of the 950 persons present at the two services, 665 surveys were completed and handed in.

There follows a copy of the survey form that was used (with certain revisions thought wise in view of some confusion noted in the responses).

Age _____   Sex _____

How long a member of Centenary United Methodist Church?

_____

Are you a regular visitor? _____ (Please check)

1. Do you attend church with frequent regularity?
   Yes _____ No _____

2. If answer to above is "YES," why do you attend church?

_____ I have an inner desire to worship.

_____ I consider public worship a duty.

_____ Because of my past training; it is a habit.

_____ I attend primarily because of the minister.

_____ I am always benefited spiritually by worship service.

_____ I want to set a good example for my children.

_____ Other

3. Do you feel that you are living a reasonably good Christian life?
   Yes _____   No _____

4. To what degree do your religious beliefs affect your daily thinking and acting?

   _____ a great deal   _____ hardly any
   _____ some   _____ not at all

5. Are you a member of any "small group" within Centenary Church?
   Yes _____   No _____

   _____ Sharing   _____ Work group
   _____ Bible study   _____ Other
   _____ Prayer

6. In your opinion, what should be the main concern of the local church? What do you want your church to help you do? (Number in order of priority, 1, 2, 3, etc.)

   _____ Be alert to needs of others in the community
   _____ Find meaning to life
   _____ Meet personal problems
   _____ Strengthen faith & devotion
   _____ Understand the Bible
   _____ Understand Christian doctrine
   _____ Give my family Christian education
   _____ Stimulate me to witnessing and evangelism
   _____ Make me concerned for world evangelization
   _____ Make me sensitive to social issues

7. When was the last time you read anything in the Bible?

   _____ today   _____ at least a year ago
   _____ last week   _____ still longer
   _____ at least a month ago   _____ do not read the Bible

8. Do you attend Sunday school weekly?
   Yes _____   No _____

9. If answer to above is "YES," why do you attend Sunday school?

   _____ The lessons help me spiritually.
   _____ I like the teacher.
   _____ I enjoy the fellowship of the class.
   _____ Other

10. If answer to above is "NO," why do you not attend Sunday school?
    Please list reasons.

    _____

    _____

    _____

11. Do you know the basic beliefs of the United Methodist Church?
    Yes _____   No _____

    Do you know what makes the United Methodist Church distinctive
    from other Protestant denominations?
    Yes _____   No _____

12. Do you read devotional literature frequently?
    Yes _____   No _____
    What type?

    _____ contemporary devotional periodicals
    _____ hymns, poems
    _____ older devotional classics
    _____ other

13. Do you have family worship? Yes _____   No _____

14. Do you pray?

    _____ regularly   _____ only in crisis situations
    _____ frequently   _____ seldom or never
    _____ occasionally

15. Why do you pray?

    _____ because it is a habit (from childhood)
    _____ because I am afraid

_____ because it eases my conscience
_____ because my prayers are often answered
_____ because it makes me feel better
_____ other
_____ because I am dependent upon God for daily help

16. Are you practicing any of the personal spiritual disciplines?

_____ Solitude—quiet time   _____ Bible Study
_____ Spiritual reflection   _____ Tithing
_____ Moderation/Abstinence   _____ Others
_____ Fasting

17. Do members of the congregation supply your need for fellowship and well-being?   Yes _____   No _____

18. If the answer to the above is "NO," where are you finding these needs met? _____
                         (identify group or organization)
_____ I am not finding it anywhere

19. Are you practicing Christian stewardship?

Time: Yes _____ No _____
Possessions: Yes _____ No _____
Talents: Yes _____ No _____
Influence: Yes _____ No _____

20. What are you now doing in Centenary Church, in addition to attending worship services and/or Sunday school?

(On the survey form devised for your church perhaps the main activities of the church should be listed here so that the respondent may check them.)

_____

_____

21. Why are you active in Centenary Church?

_____ It is a part of my commitment to Christ and the church.
_____ I am helped personally when I share in such activity.
_____ I like to work with others.
_____ Other

22. Do you talk to others about Jesus Christ and the Christian faith?

    in the home   Yes _____   No _____
    in social circles   Yes _____   No _____
    at work   Yes _____   No _____
    at play   Yes _____   No _____
    at school   Yes _____   No _____
    during leisure time Yes _____   No _____

23. Do you engage in Christian service to others?

    Personally   Yes _____   No _____
    As a member of a group or organization
    Yes _____   No _____

24. Answering this survey-questionnaire has helped me to understand my spiritual commitment and life.

    Yes _____   No _____   Don't know _____

25. I am convinced that a balanced program of spiritual formation (spiritual growth - discipleship - wholeness) will be good for Centenary Church.

    Yes _____   No _____   Have no opinion _____

The original compilation of the results of the survey was made according to age grouping. (See forms used to tabulate the results.) Perhaps some churches will be able to do both the survey and tabulate the results on computer.

At the first meeting of the planning committee both the purpose and the administrative process to be followed were outlined. The purpose of the planning committee is to devise a church-wide plan of spiritual formation suitable for immediate implementation.

Here is the administrative process that was to be followed in the planning stages:

    I. Define MISSION PURPOSE
        1. What is purpose of program?
        2. Write statement of purpose

II.　GOAL DEVELOPMENT
　　(A goal is what we want to attain as an end result.)
　　　1.　Present situation
　　　2.　Assumptions
　　　3.　Identify needs/concerns

III.　Decide on OBJECTIVES
　　(An objective is a specific target to be reached in the attainment of the goals.)
　　　1.　Prioritize objectives
　　　2.　Anticipate obstacles

IV.　Work out MISSION DESIGN
　　What are the details of the program?

V.　Decide upon MISSION MANAGEMENT
　　Who will supervise program?

VI.　Plan for IMPLEMENTATION of the program
　　Time schedule

COMPILATION OF SURVEY RESPONSES

Sex _____　　　　　　Age Grouping _____

Member of Centenary? _____

Regular visitor?　　Yes _____

　　　　　　　　　　No _____

1.　Attend frequently?

　　　　　　Yes _____

　　　　　　No _____

2.　Why attend?

　　　a. inner worship _____
　　　b. public worship _____
　　　c. habit _____
　　　d. minister _____

e. spiritually benefited _____

f. set example _____

g. other _____

3. Live good life?

Yes _____

No _____

4. Religious beliefs affect thoughts and acts?

a. great deal _____

b. some _____

c. hardly any _____

d. not at all _____

5. Member of small group?

a. sharing _____

b. Bible study _____

c. prayer _____

d. work group _____

e. other _____

6. Main concern of church?

a. spiritual life _____

b. family _____

c. evangelism _____

d. social problems _____

e. other _____

7. When last read Bible?

a. today _____

b. last week _____

c. month ago _____

d. year ago _____

e. longer _____

f. do not read _____

g. other _____

8. Attend Sunday school?

    a. yes _____

    b. no _____

9.   Why?

    a. lessons help _____

    b. fellowship _____

    c. teacher _____

    d. other _____

10. Why not? _____

11. Know UMC basic beliefs?

    yes _____

    no _____

    Know difference:

    yes _____

    no _____

12.   Read devotional literature?

    yes _____

    no _____

    Kind

    a. contemporary _____

    b. classic _____

    c. hymns _____

    d. other _____

13. Family worship?

    yes _____

    no _____

14. Do you pray?

    a. regularly _____

    b. frequently _____

    c. occasionally _____

    d. crisis _____

    e. seldom _____

    f. other _____

15. Why?

    a. habit _____

    b. conscience _____

    c. feels better _____

    d. dependent upon God _____

    e. fear _____

    f. answered prayers _____

    g. other _____

16. Spiritual disciplines?

    a. quiet time _____

    b. reflection _____

    c. abstinence _____

    d. fasting _____

    e. study _____

    f. tithing _____

    g. other _____

17. Fellowship? _____

    yes _____

    no _____

18. Where needs met?

    _____

    Nowhere _____

19. Christian stewardship?

    a. time _____

    b. talents _____

    c. possessions _____

    d. influence _____

    e. other _____

20. Activities? _____

_____

21. Why active?

    a. commitment _____

    b. personal help _____

    c. work with others _____

    d. other _____

22. Talk to others about Jesus?

    a. home _____

    b. work _____

    c. school _____

    d. social circles _____

    e. play _____

    f. leisure time _____

    g. other _____

23. Christian service?

    a. personally _____

    b. part of group _____

24. Understand commitment

    yes _____

    no _____

    don't know _____

25. Spiritual formation good?

    yes _____

    no _____

    no opinion _____

DEVELOPMENT

The first meeting of the planning committee centered on the development of a statement of purpose for the church-wide program of spiritual formation. The group gave its attention to developing the assumptions which now undergird the program of spiritual formation in Centenary Church. These assumptions were based on the interpretation of the results of the survey taken among the congregation.

The following five assumptions were accepted:

1. Members need to be developed spiritually, psychologically, and socially.
2. It is believed that a program of spiritual formation will be good for the church.
3. Wholeness, which is the objective of spiritual formation, includes the total person.
4. Persons want to be ministered to, integrated, and made whole.
5. The body of Christ provides the primary means through which the grace of God is expressed; therefore, a balanced, structured, flexible program of spiritual formation is legitimate for individuals, the church, and the community.

The second meeting dealt with the development of mission goals and objectives. As expected, needs were apparent in every area. More people need to be studying the Bible and helped to apply biblical teachings to everyday life. Church members need to learn the meaning of prayer and to develop satisfying times and patterns of personal devotion. Christian stewardship must be seen as more far-reaching than merely a regular financial contribution to the church through a personal check or the use of church envelopes. The talents of professing Christians must be employed for the glory of Christ through the church.

Few professing Christians participate in any continuing type of evangelism. The Christian nurture of the family is imperative. Far too few church members either understand the meaning of Christian community or participate in therapeutic Christian fellowship. United Methodists have been challenged to theologize, but few really understand the basics of the Christian faith or the theological distinctives of their own denomination. The meaning of corporate worship must be rediscovered. A contemporary writer speaks of worship as the "missing jewel" in today's evangelical churches. At the third meeting, we focused on the initial design. What should be the content of an adequate church-wide plan of spiritual formation? The committee agreed that an ideal plan should include ten areas. Here is a list of them and a descriptive statement about the purpose of each area.

1. BIBLE STUDY—taking advantage of opportunities to study God's Word in order to be guided in wholesome spiritual growth.

2. THEOLOGICAL STUDY—gaining an understanding of the essentials of the Christian faith and the distinctive doctrines of Methodism.

3. DEVOTIONAL LITERATURE—developing one's personal devotional life through a study of the writings of the spiritual leaders of the Christian centuries.

4. PRAYER—learning how to pray and to practice prayer.

5. SPIRITUAL DISCIPLINES—practicing disciplined living as the divinely appointed means of spiritual growth.

6. COMMUNITY—learning that we need one another in the process of spiritual growth and how to build community in the body of Christ.

7. STEWARDSHIP—understanding and demonstrating the lordship of Jesus Christ over all aspects of one's life.

8. WITNESSING and EVANGELISM—enabling the born-again Christian to experience spiritual growth through personal obedience to Christ's Great Commission.

9. SERVICE—manifesting the servant stance of Jesus Christ as the evidence of spiritual growth.

10. PSYCHO-SOCIAL GROWTH—using the insights of psychology and sociology as means to enhance the spiritual life of individuals and through them the family and community.

The planning committee decided that the most practical way for recommendations to be made concerning the specific content of each of the ten areas would be to divide into ten subcommittees, each group consisting of those personally interested in the specific area under consideration.

As a result of extensive homework, many recommendations relating to each of the areas were presented. Here is a sampling:

BIBLE STUDY

1. Organize a class for leaders of small groups to learn methods of Bible study
2. Form classes and small groups for Bible study
3. Provide video tapes series relative to the use of the Bible
4. Recommend Bible studies by the minister at Sunday evening services
5. Devise a method to help people study the Bible on their own

THEOLOGICAL STUDY

Form theological study classes

1. to study basic Christian theology
2. to study the theology of Methodism
3. to concentrate on specialized theological studies
    a. the nature of God
    b. theologians of the centuries
    c. contemporary theologians
    d. practical theological questions that Christians ask

DEVOTIONAL LITERATURE

1. Provide bibliography of devotional literature
2. Provide bookrack containing devotional literature in narthex of church
3. Increase number of devotional books in church library
4. Have classes in devotional classics

PRAYER

1. Form classes to study nature and methods of prayer
2. Establish more prayer groups
3. Devise system of prayer partners
4. Have prayer time before the Sunday evening service
5. Hold all-night prayer vigils

SPIRITUAL DISCIPLINES

1. Encourage private practice of spiritual disciplines

   2. Form small covenant groups for the practice of disciplines
   3. Ask the pastors to preach occasional sermons/messages on disciplines
   4. Have weekend seminars/workshops on the disciplines
   5. Emphasize a specific discipline each month at the church

COMMUNITY

   1. Make available more small-group experiences in community
   2. Focus on building community in Sunday school classes and in different work areas
   3. Have intergenerational retreats centered on spiritual formation
   4. Enroll new members in community-building experiences

STEWARDSHIP

   1. Have effective method of follow-up of annual stewardship survey of members
   2. Have every new member participate at once in a personal stewardship survey
   3. Set up classes in the meaning and practice of Christian stewardship
   4. Encourage Sunday school classes to deal with responsibility for total stewardship

WITNESSING AND EVANGELISM

   1. Plan church-wide revival services
   2. Provide for lay witnessing from the pulpit
   3. Establish a Christian drama group
   4. Organize witness teams for continuing ministry
   5. Have witnessing visits to hospitals, nursing homes, prisons

SERVICE

   1. Coordinate the more than 140 opportunities for service within Centenary's present ministry
   2. Seek every opportunity for new avenues of service and enlist and train workers

PSYCHO-SOCIAL DEVELOPMENT

Have classes/small groups that deal with such areas as:

1. Personality inventory
2. Self-esteem
3. Destructive emotions
4. Depression/anxiety
5. Stress
6. Moral development
7. Marriage enrichment
8. Family enrichment
9. Sexuality
10. Gerontology
11. Death
12. Wholeness

All of these recommendations were to be reported later to the leaders and support teams were set up to administer each area in the church-wide plan of spiritual formation. This procedure will become clearer in the discussion of Mission Management which follows.

MISSION MANAGEMENT

An important meeting of the planning committee dealt with Mission Management. How will each area in the program be constituted? What kind of supervisory organization is needed for each area? For the program as a whole? What is a practical schedule for the implementation of the program initially?

It was decided that the program in each area of spiritual formation, i.e., Bible study, theological study, devotional literature, prayer, spiritual disciplines, community, stewardship, witnessing and evangelism, service, and psycho-social growth should be planned in detail by a lay assistant (or assistants) in consultation with a support team of carefully selected individuals who have a special interest in the particular area. (It was agreed that no person should serve on more than one support team in the program.)

The lay assistant(s) will be directly responsible to the director of the program, who in the Centenary Model was the Minister of Spiritual Formation.

As the plan was developed in each of the areas under the leadership of the lay assistant(s), the planning committee served as the approving body and the liaison with the church officiary.

SPIRITUAL FORMATION ORGANIZATIONAL CHART

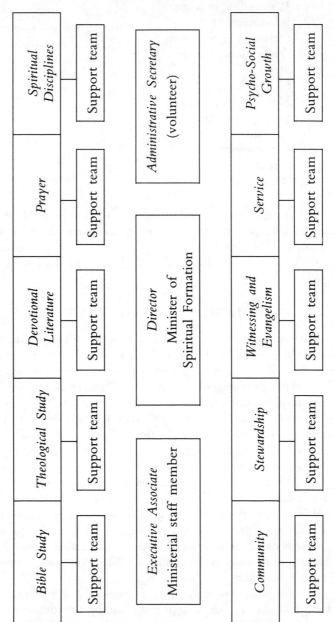

The next step, then, was to choose the lay assistants. This was done in consultation with the senior minister. Criteria for selection included: (1) personal spiritual dedication and concern for spiritual formation; (2) known interest and proved experience in the particular area; (3) interest already shown in the development of this new church-wide program of spiritual formation; (4) willingness to make the new assignment a priority even if it means giving up previously held assignments.

When the lay assistants had been chosen and had agreed to serve, they were given the opportunity of choosing their support team, the number of members being entirely up to them. In some instances only one or two served on the support team. In the area of prayer an entire work area became the support team.

The work of actually constituting the program in each area of spiritual formation had now begun. The director met with each lay assistant(s) and support team in order to discuss program possibilities within each area and to decide upon what would be done initially. The actual results of this process will be presented in the next chapter when we discuss how the Centenary Model was implemented.

The previous paragraphs describe the participants in the Mission Management of the church-wide plan being developed. The organizational chart (p.   ) shows how it all fits together. Keep in mind that the total management of the plan was actually under the governance and surveillance of a continuing planning committee.

MISSION IMPLEMENTATION

A further decision that had to be made by the planning committee was the setting of an actual date for the beginning of the church-wide program of spiritual formation. Two things were involved here: (1) the best time to present it to the congregation and ask for signing of covenant cards; (2) the amount of time needed between the signing of the covenant cards by the members of the congregation and the actual beginning of participation in the program. In the case of Centenary, a month and a half proved to be the interim period. The next chapter tells the story of the implementation details in the Centenary Model.

SUMMARY

Suggested Schedule for Initial Meetings of Planning Committee

1st Meeting—Mission Purpose

2nd Meeting—Mission Goals and Objectives

3rd and 4th Meetings—Mission Design
(and further meetings if necessary)

Next Meeting—Mission Management

Next Meeting—Mission Implementation

7

THE CENTENARY MODEL
HOW IT WAS IMPLEMENTED

When the program plans had been completed in each of the areas included in the church-wide plan of spiritual formation at Centenary Church, the two worship services on a designated Sunday morning became the opportunity both to announce what was being offered in spiritual formation and to give the members of the congregation the occasion to signify their intention to participate.

As the Minister of Spiritual Formation on the church staff, I preached the sermon and announced the plan to the congregation. My subject was "Stamp Thine Own Image on My Heart," and I used the text in 2 Peter 3:18 (RSV)—"Grow in grace and in the knowledge of our Lord and Savior Jesus Christ."

The sermon built upon the assumption that Christian growth, discipleship, spiritual formation is the crying need of individuals, local churches, and entire denominations. Results of recent religious surveys were used to document such an assumption. A descriptive analysis of spiritual formation in general was presented (see chapters 1 and 5), together with a reference to the imperatives of spiritual formation (see chapter 4).

I closed with an appeal for all to take advantage of the opportunities for spiritual growth that were being offered within the local church. Covenant cards were distributed and members of the congregation were given opportunity to sign them before the end of the service.

CENTENARY UNITED METHODIST CHURCH

Lexington, Kentucky

MY PERSONAL COVENANT

_____ I desire to participate in the program of Spiritual Formation now being offered at Centenary United Methodist Church

My present interests are in the following areas (check #1, #2, #3, in order of personal priority):

_____ Bible Study   _____ Community

_____ Theological Study   _____ Stewardship

_____ Devotional Literature _____ Witnessing/
                                          Evangelism

_____ Prayer   _____ Service

_____ Spiritual Disciplines _____ Psycho-Social Growth

Name _____ Date _____
            (Please Print)

Address _____ Telephone _____

Approximately one-half of those present at the two worship services returned a signed covenant card. The breakdown of the first choices of preference is interesting:

Bible Study	182	Community	18
Theological Study	37	Stewardship	9
Devotional Literature	39	Witnessing/Evangelism	14
Prayer	55	Service	34
Spiritual Disciplines	37	Psycho-Social Growth	36

At the beginning of the implementation of this new program, only the first choices were collated. Lists of names and addresses of respondents in each of the areas were drawn up. Within a reasonably short time a letter was sent to each person who had signed a covenant card, informing each of opportunities available in the area of one's first choice.

Here are samples of the forms we enclosed in the letter. Each person received only one enclosure.

SPIRITUAL FORMATION

Area: Bible Study

Purpose: To take advantage of opportunities to study God's Word in order to be guided in wholesome spiritual growth.

Opportunities for Spiritual Formation in this area:
(Check only *one*.)

_____ Bible study for new Christians.

_____ Small groups for Bible studies (beginning, intermediated, advanced).

_____ Survey of the Bible.

_____ Wednesday night Bible studies at church (6:30 or 7:30).

_____ Training class in leadership of Bible study groups.

Name _____ Telephone _____

SPIRITUAL FORMATION

Area: Theological Study

Purpose: To gain an understanding of the essentials of the Christian faith and the distinctive doctrines of Methodism.

Opportunities for Spiritual Formation in this area:
(Check only *one*.)

_____ Basic theological studies.

_____ The theology of Methodism.

_____ Theological discussion group.

_____ The Holy Spirit (Koinonia classroom: Sundays, May 1, 8, 15, 22, 29; 9:50 a.m.).

Name _____ Telephone _____

SPIRITUAL FORMATION

Area: Devotional Literature

Purpose: To develop your personal devotional life through a study of the writings of the spiritual leaders of the Christian centuries.

Opportunities for Spiritual Formation in this area:
(Check only *one*.)

_____ A survey of devotional literature.

_____ In-depth study of selected devotional writings.

_____ The family's use of devotional literature.

_____ How to share devotional literature with shut-ins.

Name _____ Telephone _____

SPIRITUAL FORMATION

Area: Prayer

Purpose: In the spirit of a true disciple of Christ, to learn how to pray and to practice prayer.

Opportunities for Spiritual Formation in this area:
(Check only *one*.)

_____ Class on the meaning and methods of prayer.

_____ Intercessory prayer groups.

_____ Prayer teams to visit the shut-ins.

Name _____ Telephone _____

SPIRITUAL FORMATION

Area: Spiritual Disciplines

Purpose: To discover the practice of disciplined living as the divinely appointed means of spiritual.

Opportunities for Spiritual Formation in this area:
(Check only *one*.)

_____ Study of Richard Foster's book, *Celebration or Discipline*.

_____ Four-month designed experiment in disciplined living.

Name _____ Telephone _____

SPIRITUAL FORMATION

Area: Community

Purpose: To learn that we need one another in the process of spiritual growth and to build community in the body of Christ.

Opportunities for Spiritual Formation in this area:
(Check only *one*.)

_____ Groups for study, sharing, and support (nature of community, personal needs, mutual support).

_____ Study of practical ways of building community.

_____ Study of corporate spiritual disciplines.

Name _____ Telephone _____

SPIRITUAL FORMATION

Area: Stewardship

Purpose: To understand and demonstrate the lordship of Jesus Christ over all aspects of your life.

Opportunities for Spiritual Formation in this area:
(Check only *one*.)

_____ Class on the meaning of Christian stewardship.

_____ Workshop on Christian financial planning.

Name _____ Telephone _____

SPIRITUAL FORMATION

Area: Witnessing/Evangelism

Purpose: For the "born again" Christian to experience spiritual growth through personal obedience to Christ's Great Commission.

Opportunities for Spiritual Formation in this area:
(Check only *one*.)

_____ Class—the meaning and practice of evangelism.

_____ Visitation teams.

_____ Drama group.

Name _____ Telephone _____

SPIRITUAL FORMATION

Area: Service

Purpose: To manifest the "servant stance" of Jesus Christ as the evidence of spiritual growth.

Opportunities for Spiritual Formation in this area:
(Check only *one*.)

_____ Serving individuals in need (transportation, personal care, house and yard duties).

_____ Serving persons in nursing homes.

_____ Ministering through Prison Fellowship.

_____ Sign language ministry.

_____ Ministering at Nathaniel Mission.

_____ Ministry through Community Volunteers.

Name _____ Telephone _____

SPIRITUAL FORMATION

Area: Psycho-Social Growth

Purpose: To use the insights of psychology and sociology as a means to enhance the spiritual life of individuals and through them the family and community.

Opportunities for Spiritual Formation in this area:
(Check order of preference — 1, 2, 3)

_____ Personality (Meyers-Briggs Type Indicator)

_____ Self-Esteem

_____ Inner Conflict/Anger

_____ Moral Development

_____ Life's Cycles

Name _____ Telephone _____

As the responses were returned, telling which opportunity one wanted in one's area of first choice, the administrative secretary began the task of making assignments. Lists containing accurate information were sent to each of the lay assistants so that persons enrolling in a particular area could be notified by them. Plans were then completed for special activities in each of the areas.

As the studies and activities continued in the various areas, the supervision of the total program was being cared for. The lay assistant(s) was (were) directly responsible to the director, and a monthly report was asked for. (See forms on following pages.) There was also a monthly meeting of all the lay assistants with the director.

SPIRITUAL FORMATION

Activities Report

Area ———————————————————

Lay Assistants(s) ————————————————— Date ————

1. Changes in support team (list both cancellations and additions).

2. Action(s) taken by support team or lay assistant(s). Include decisions regarding publicity, policy, dividing of responsibilities, etc.

3. Current activities (by name of activity). For new listings, give name of leader, name of activity, materials being used, and list of participants.

4. Activities planned (give meeting time and place, beginning date, expected duration, leader, materials to be used).

5. Membership changes
    A. Changes in class or activity leaders
    B. Changes in class or activity membership (give name of participant, name of activity, and whether a cancellation or addition).
    C. Changes in area membership (give name of participant, current area, new area being added or changed to).

The lay assistants were asked to provide in advance the information to be included on the monthly church calendar (see form on p. 100).

SPIRITUAL FORMATION

Monthly Report of Lay Assistant(s)

To: Frank Bateman Stanger, Director

From: _____   Lay Assistant(s)

Area _____   Date: _____ 1983

I. Activities During Past Month

    1. Classes (list separately, including name of leader and average attendance)

    _____

    _____

    _____

    2. Activities other than classes
    (List separately, including name of leader and average number of participants.)

    _____

    _____

    _____

II. Are you discovering areas of weakness in your program that need to be dealt with? (List)

    _____

    _____

    _____

SPIRITUAL FORMATION

Calendar Information

For the Month of _____, 19 ____

AREA: _____   (For information: _____)

Time   Event   Place

....

Mondays:

....

Tuesdays:

....

Wednesdays:

....

Thursdays:

....

Fridays:

....

Saturdays:

....

Other Events:

....

Submitted by _____ Date _____

The planning committee became aware of the growing pains in a new church-wide plan of spiritual formation and endeavored to deal wisely with both problems and opportunities within the first year of the operation of the plan.

It became evident that the following issues would have to be dealt with, sooner or later:

1. Competition for time with an already crowded church schedule
2. The misconception of "competition" with other programs. Spiritual formation has to be seen as a coordinating rather than a competing emphasis
3. How and when participants in spiritual formation are to be shifted to new foci within a chosen area, and when they should be encouraged to move into another area just as important for spiritual growth
4. Ways to develop a sense of commitment within the participants
5. Ways to provide for continuing leadership in the programs
6. The best way to evaluate the program, how soon and how often it should be done

An administrative technique that proved of inestimable help and support to the director was the creation of an executive committee which usually met weekly. In addition to the director, the executive committee consisted of the associate minister of the church and a talented volunteer who served as administrative secretary. Both of these persons provided wise counsel to the director, and the administrative secretary rendered incalculable service by taking care of all the paperwork involved.

I must say a word about finances. The spiritual formation program requested separate funds in the church budget. Even though these were limited, they met a definite need in the operation of the program. The only subsidies to the leaders, provided by the budget, were in the area of providing teaching materials, the services of the church office, and postage. Each person enrolled in the program bore personally the expense for any materials used in group activities.

In this and the preceding chapter, I have endeavored to

LINCOLN CHRISTIAN COLLEGE AND SEMINARY

present the actual picture of the creation and implementation of a church-wide plan of spiritual formation in a particular church. Building upon the experience of the Centenary Model, the next chapter will outline both general principles and offer detailed suggestions for developing a plan of spiritual formation in any local church.

8

DEVELOPING A PLAN FOR YOUR CHURCH

The opening section of this book focused upon both the nature and importance of spiritual formation for a Christian person and for the church. The next section outlined step by step how an actual plan of spiritual formation was developed and implemented in a local church.

Now it would seem practical in this closing section to outline the steps for developing a plan of spiritual formation in a local church, whatever size or wherever situated, building upon the experience of the Centenary Model.

PREPARATION

Adequate preparation is necessary for any activity which is intended to be sustained. Whenever a necessary stage in preparation is bypassed the planned activity is in danger of either total collapse or inefficient operation.

Adequate preparation for the development of a church-wide plan of spiritual formation includes (1) comprehension, (2) conviction, (3) ability to counter inbred resistance.

Comprehension

First of all, at the very beginning, the nature of spiritual formation and its objectives must be clearly understood. So often as I conduct church seminars in spiritual formation, I am immediately confronted with a statement something like this: "Please tell us what you mean by spiritual formation." Then sometimes the comment is added, "We never heard the term before."

Don't expect to get off the ground in planning unless you help people understand at the very beginning exactly what is being talked about. Chapter 1 talks about both the background and meaning of the term. I hope that what is written there will be helpful as a local church begins to consider the development of a plan for the spiritual growth of its members.

There must also be an understanding of the imperatives and objectives of a plan of spiritual formation. Here the reader is referred to chapter 4.

Conviction

Adequate comprehension must lead to conviction if a church-wide plan is to develop. There needs to be both the personal conviction of responsible individuals and the corporate conviction of responsible church bodies that spiritual formation must become a priority in the program of the total church. The senior minister of a church must be convinced of the need for spiritual formation in his congregation. The associate minister(s) must also be convinced. And, if perchance, a senior minister asks an associate or assistant minister to head up such a plan in the church, the associate or assistant must be convinced not only of the validity of spiritual formation but also that spiritual formation in the church is a top priority in the mind of the senior minister.

Every member of the ministerial staff must be convinced of the basic importance of spiritual formation. The plan will never develop fully or work if the minister of Christian education, or the minister of evangelism, or the minister of youth, or the minister of music, or any other ranking member of the staff sees spiritual formation as institutionally competitive or as an intrusion upon another's turf.

Members of the governing body of a local church and of other high ranking boards/councils/commissions/committees must become convinced and pledge their wholehearted support to such an undertaking. Just so, leaders in the other areas of the church's life—men's work, women's work, youth work, senior citizens, etc.—must be helped to see how a plan of spiritual formation fits meaningfully into the total work of the church.

I must also add that there needs to be a vital conviction of the significance of a church-wide plan of spiritual formation on the part of those persons in the membership of the church who are already participating in spiritual formation activities in one way or another—e.g., covenant groups, prayer groups, disciplined cells, and the like.

During the earliest stages in the development of a church-wide plan, those who are active in such an undertaking must be willing to spend all the time necessary to help others both comprehend and become convinced. To pass such an initial state before it is fulfilled adequately may result in heartbreaking frustrations.

Ability to Counter Resistance

We must recognize and deal with the reasons for initial resistance to the development of a church-wide plan of spiritual formation. We have already implied ignorance in some quarters about the meaning of it all. But there can also be prejudice—not wanting a local church to be considered too pious—or the fear that spiritual formation is overly individualistic to the neglect of proper social concerns.

There is also the possibility of resistance in relation to certain so-called spiritual concerns. Some are quick to ask, "Is not an organized, structured, supervised plan for spiritual growth in contradiction to the spontaneity of the Holy Spirit at work in persons?" "And what about discipline (which is so unappealing to so many)? Is it not an antithesis to the direct operation of God's grace within a person's life?"

So, the stage of preparation must be dealt with and fulfilled as the initial process in the establishment of a church-wide plan of spiritual formation.

PLANNING

In developing a program of spiritual formation in a local church, we build upon the assumption that organization and structure are essential. Whence arose the erroneous myth that planning is legitimate in every area except the spiritual?

Everything in God's universe speaks of planning. We can predict accurately the time of the sunrise and the sunset tomorrow. Season always follows season. The exact moment of a solar or lunar eclipse is predictable. Geology is a study of the divine plan in the rocky structure of the earth. The sciences of zoology and biology reveal the divine plan in animal and human life. Botany is the study of the cosmic structure of beauty and fruitfulness in plant life. The law of the harvest is an eloquent confirmation of God's planning in the physical earth: the seed—the blade—the ear—the full corn in the ear. Whatever is sown is reaped.

God has implanted the secret of planning in the minds of humans. The social, political, economic, and ecclesiastical worlds depend upon effective organization. Study an organizational chart of an industry or a business. Look at the constitution and laws of the United States government. Review the book of discipline of your own particular church denomination.

I am writing these lines after returning a few days ago from an Alaskan cruise on the *Nieuw Amsterdam,* nearly 34,000 tons and carrying 1,160 passengers and employing a crew of perhaps 400. From the moment of embarkation to that of disembarkation, every detail of the 2000-mile, 7-day trip was planned and carried through with almost flawless accuracy. The entire event could never have happened without such planning and organization.

And what about space explorations? Can we even imagine the planning that goes into each successful adventure into space? So accurate is it all that recently even four seconds before countdown spelled the difference between success and failure.

Just so, in the area of spiritual activities, careful planning is essential. Here we are dependent not only upon the genius of creative minds, but also upon the inspiration and guidance of the Holy Spirit. Here are the important items to be on the planning agenda:

1. *Mission Statement* (purpose, objectives, and goals): What is the purpose of a church-wide plan of spiritual formation? What are the hoped-for accomplishments of such a program?

2. *Mission Program*: What are the specific needs in the area of spiritual formation in a particular local church? (These are discovered most effectively through a church-wide survey. See chapter 6.) Which of the ten essential areas in spiritual formation

should be given priority in the plan being developed for a particular congregation?

For purposes of clarity at this point, here is a recapitulation of each of the areas essential to spiritual formation:

1. BIBLE STUDY—taking advantage of opportunities to study God's Word in order to be guided in wholesome spiritual growth

2. THEOLOGICAL STUDY—gaining an understanding of the essentials of the Christian faith and the distinctive doctrines of one's denomination

3. DEVOTIONAL LITERATURE—developing one's personal devotional life through a study of the writings of spiritual leaders of the Christian centuries

4. PRAYER—Learning how to pray and to practice prayer

5. SPIRITUAL DISCIPLINES—practicing disciplined living as the divinely appointed means of spiritual growth

6. COMMUNITY—learning that we need one another in the process of spiritual growth and ways to build community in the body of Christ

7. STEWARDSHIP—understanding and demonstrating the lordship of Jesus Christ over all aspects of one's life

8. WITNESSING AND EVANGELISM—enabling the born-again Christian to experience spiritual growth through personal obedience to Christ's Great Commission

9. SERVICE—manifesting the servant stance of Jesus Christ as the evidence of spiritual growth

10. PSYCHO-SOCIAL GROWTH—using the insights of psychology and sociology as a means to enhance the spiritual life of individuals and through them the family and community

It may not be practical for a local church to begin with all ten areas, however important each is. Therefore, in the planning process it must be decided which areas should have priority and which emphases are most congenial to that local congregation in the light of existing circumstances.

A basic premise of planning, from a Christian perspective, is to make people objects rather than subjects in the planning. The all-important issue is this: What is good for the spiritual growth of persons in this particular congregation? Planning is community-oriented rather than primarily individualistic.

3. *Coordination*: One of the lessons learned the hard way in the Centenary experience is the necessity of understanding spiritual formation in its coordinating role. There must be a willingness to coordinate the present church program in its manifold aspects with the objectives of spiritual formation.

In view of the inevitable overlapping of current church programs with a new overall plan of spiritual formation being introduced, the first reaction may be that of competition. For illustration, the work area on education is already busily engaged in promoting a wholesome program of teaching, study, and Christian nurture. But here comes a new program of spiritual formation with its emphasis on Bible study, theological study, devotional studies, and studies planned in other areas. At first sight this may appear as competition, with the new competing with the old.

I know that I am repeating myself here, but it is essential in the planning process to clear the air about this matter of competition. In no way is spiritual formation competing with any other activity in the church which contributes to spiritual growth. The true picture must be seen. Every legitimate activity in the church ought to be focused on spiritual growth. A master plan of spiritual formation seeks to coordinate all these activities under the umbrella of achieving the true objective of the church. The spiritual formation emphasis in a local church seeks to insure that the church never loses its true perspective of spirituality.

Take an average local church with its emphases upon worship, education, stewardship, evangelism, service and social action. Every one of these areas is indissolubly related to spiritual formation. Worship, Christian education, and the practice of stewardship are essential to spiritual growth. Evangelism and service and social action are the inevitable manifestations of growth in the lives of Christians.

4. *Mission Management*: There must also be careful planning

in relation to the management of the program of spiritual formation. Who will supervise the total program? Who will serve as the director of spiritual formation in the church? Should it be the senior minister? A member of the clerical staff? A layperson? This will have to be decided in the light of the circumstances in a particular church. If the minister is not the director of spiritual formation, then the relationship of the director to the minister must be worked out carefully.

Will there be a special committee/task force of representative church members who will provide a continuing liaison between the spiritual formation program and the church officiary? Will official representatives of spiritual formation sit on the administrative board/general council of the church? What will be the plan of reporting to the church officiary?

Who will assist the director of the program? How will the leaders in each of the areas be chosen? Who will have final authority in the selection of teachers and groups leaders and in the choosing of particular studies/activities? Who will be responsible for the evaluation of the program as it progresses? All of these management concerns must be settled in advance of the implementation of the program.

Committees and commissions whose objective is to aid in both the development and manifestation of spirituality in the lives of church members are all arms of an overall program of spiritual formation. How much more effective it is when all these related activities are coordinated. An apt illustration is in the area of service. We discovered in Centenary Church that at any given time there are at least 140 opportunities for service. If the administration of all of these were coordinated, every one would be fulfilled in one way or another, and much wasted effort would be avoided.

In addition to the need of coordination in relation to official church structure and programs, there must also be coordination with any non-official groups in the church which are active in spiritual formation. Many churches have groups of concerned laypersons, outside the regularly organized committees and work areas, who have banded themselves together for purposes of spiritual growth. Such groups must immediately be made a part of the total spiritual formation efforts.

I am convinced that the key to the coordination process is the minister of the church. He is in a strategic position to interpret the objectives of spiritual formation to all those who lead in the various aspects of the church's program and to assist them and their associates in achieving the needed coordination.

Such church-wide coordination is essential if a program of spiritual formation is to be effective in a local church. Norman Shawchuck, a denominational leader in spiritual formation, has said, "My greatest fear is that spiritual formation will not be integrated into the total life of the church, including management and administration."

5. *Mission Implementation*: The planning process also determines the specific details, such as dates and initial procedures, in the implementation of the church-wide plan of spiritual formation. Naturally, the actual implementation will be determined by the satisfactory completion of all the necessary steps in the preparation/planning stages. The program must be in place, personnel selected for its management, and actual communication with the congregation must be in progress. (The next section will deal more specifically with this important area of communication.)

In the planning for mission-implementation, it must be decided when and how the program of spiritual formation will be presented to the congregation as a whole. Also, it must be determined in what specific manner the members will be given an opportunity to express the desire to participate.

I recommend using the Sunday worship services for the launching of the new program and the use of a specially prepared covenant card for the congregation to declare their intentions (see chapter 7).

PARTICIPATION

A third stage in the development of a church-wide program of spiritual formation is that of participation. Participation is here spoken of in one of its more theoretical aspects, that of sharing and communication. Actually, communication and participation are closely related. When communication is effective people inevitably begin to participate, at least in their minds and emotional attachments.

Far too often programs in our churches have either failed or have operated in a mediocre manner because there was not adequate communication before the program was launched. It was assumed wrongly that merely because a minister or a prominent church leader or even a select committee decided something was going to be done, that it would inevitably succeed. But such is usually not the case.

However carefully and brilliantly a proposal may be developed, it will probably fall flat on its face unless the people for whom it is intended are prepared to receive it and participate in it. Such preparation of the congregation is accomplished through adequate communication. So while the planning committee is busily engaged in working out the details of the plan of spiritual formation, effective communication about what is going on and what is to be expected needs to be made with the members of the church.

It is imperative that this adequate communication relate to the following concerns: (1) The meaning of spiritual formation and its goals (see chapter 1); (2) why spiritual formation is imperative for the Christian (see chapter 4); (3) ways a church-wide plan of spiritual formation relates to the total program of the church (see previous section on coordination in this chapter); (4) the actual plans in spiritual formation for this particular church (see previous section on mission program in this chapter); (5) what it will mean to become involved in a continuing program of spiritual formation (see later section on commitment in this chapter).

How is effective communication about spiritual formation to be carried on? Here is a list of several valuable channels and means of communication in a local church:

1. The planning committee should make regular reports to official church groups, such as administrative board/council on ministries and work areas/commissions/committees.

2. The minister should preach a series of sermons on the general theme of spiritual growth.

3. From the pulpit the minister may make occasional reference regarding events behind the scenes in the planning for spiritual formation and what can be expected as a result of the planning.

4. Publish a series of articles on spiritual formation in a local church newspaper. In the "Centenary Experience," I wrote a series of such articles dealing with the meaning and importance of spiritual formation, how the church was developing a church-wide plan of spiritual formation, and what was to be offered in each of the essential areas.

5. A general outline of the plan of spiritual formation in process of development should be presented to every group in the church. No organization should be omitted in such a presentation. Various members of the planning committee could be assigned the responsibility of telling the story to designated groups.

6. An occasional mention of the program from the pulpit by the director, or some active lay person, should be made from time to time. The best visibility is always personal.

7. Seminars in spiritual formation could be held for interested persons who are sincerely desirous of learning about the program. One effective format for such seminars is to consider the various areas involved in spiritual formation. The entire group could consider all the areas and then report back to the total group. (See Appendix A.)

8. As soon as possible a printed brochure describing the church-wide plan of spiritual formation should be prepared and distributed to the people. Especially should this be done for those who are joining the church. (See Appendix B.)

PROCEDURES

When the planning process has been completed satisfactorily, implement the church-wide programs of spiritual formation. Such implementation includes (1) a public presentation of the total program; (2) an opportunity for interested persons to sign up for designated areas in the program; (3) the scheduling of the various classes/activities in the church program at the best times possible.

The previous chapter tells how the Centenary Model was implemented. Undoubtedly variations in the procedures will be necessary in conformity with local church circumstances, but the stages outlined in the implementation procedures seem to be valid in any situation.

Once the program of spiritual formation has been implemented, regularly provide information about the exact times and locations of various events in the developing program of spiritual formation offered in the church.

PROGRESSION

Progress is the normal mood of any program deemed worthy for a local church. The initial stages of the program must be consolidated, and every phase of the program must be stimulated to unfold with enthusiastic activity and meaningful participation. Progression requires *supervision*. The director is responsible for the total program. He or she must be accessible at all times to all those who are assisting in its leadership. The director should meet regularly with those in charge of each of the areas. The lay assistant(s) should also meet regularly with those who are leading the classes and activities. It will be helpful for the support teams in the various areas also to meet regularly with the lay assistant(s). Regular meetings of the overall administrative group provide a channel of effective contact with the total church program.

Adequate training sessions should be provided for new leaders being recruited for the program. In the Centenary Model we decided to have quarterly workshops for new leaders. The purpose of such training is to foster Christlike leadership in individuals. Possible topics to be covered during the workshops include helps in knowing Christ better, prayer, basic theological materials, church structure, personality awareness, setting realistic goals, communications and listening skills, and parliamentary procedure.

Progression is dependent upon the *commitment* of both those supervising and those being supervised. Speaking generally, the lack of commitment is one of the tragic weaknesses in the life of the church today. Commitment means pledging or engaging one's total self to a specific cause or activity. It involves binding one's self to the fulfillment of one's promise of loyalty. Just as in a pecuniary sense, commitment means handing over something of value to another for safekeeping, so in a spiritual sense commitment means binding one's self, one's loyalty, one's strength to that which results in the safekeeping and development of one's highest self.

Too often in church life vows of loyalty are kept only when it is convenient to do so. Other interests are permitted to crowd out what should be the central focus of one's attention. Frequently the full potential of the church's influence is prevented because of the less than wholehearted responses of church members.

Personal commitment is at the heart of any effective program of spiritual formation. The senior minister and church staff must be committed to spiritual formation. The officiary of the church must be committed. All those serving in leadership capacities in any area must be committed. The members of the general committee that oversees the program of spiritual formation, those who supervise the different areas, those who are responsible for groups and activities—all must be conscientiously committed to the program.

Especially is commitment necessary on the part of those who enroll in the program. Spiritual growth is not a hit-or-miss proposition. It is sequential, responding to continuing stimuli. Faithfulness in participation is imperative.

As we began to evaluate the program at Centenary, we struggled with this matter of the lack of commitment in certain areas. It was especially manifest in erratic attendance. It became evident that somehow we had to introduce the "covenant principle" into what we were doing. The element of accountability in one form or another is necessary.

It may be helpful to consider the actual proposal in this area that was adopted at Centenary:

A. No group shall function without some sort of covenant.

B. Each lay assistant will be responsible to develop an appropriate covenant for the group (or help the leaders of smaller groups to do so).
   1. We suggest that a written sheet be prepared with a statement such as, "I think the minimum we should agree upon is . . . . What do you think?" Then the group can agree on the guidelines, or terms of the covenant, and any changes can be made on their sheets. Each person should keep the sheet in a prominent place.

2. Suggest that when possible the covenant terms be given to individuals before the first meeting so they can be thinking about what they are willing to commit themselves to.

C. Each lay assistant or group leader will be responsible for the accountability to the covenant.

D. In the leadership training workshops, topics on covenanting should be included, e.g., the biblical basis of covenanting, the benefits of covenanting to both the individual and the group, practical ideas for presentation of the covenant to an individual or group.

E. A bibliography on the concept of covenanting will be made available.

It is often said that the secret of commitment is spirituality. Those who hunger and thirst after righteousness are faithful in their quest for satisfaction. Such faithfulness is always rewarded: "Blessed are those who hunger and thirst for righteousness, *for* they will be filled."

Undoubtedly, spirituality is the key issue. Spiritual formation is both dependent upon spirituality and is responsible for intensifying spiritual appetite and thirst. The development of a sense of spirituality is no easy assignment, but included in the assignment is the insistence that church membership must be primarily qualitative, not merely quantitative. The important question is not "how many members," but "what kind of members." A leader in the United Methodist Kentucky Annual Conference used to comment that it was more important to weigh sheep than merely to count them.

So the programs of spiritual formation and evangelism become indissolubly related in the life of the local church. New members who are spiritually minded must be sought. Should not an experience of the new birth be the primary condition of entrance into church membership? And such spiritually-minded members must be aided in the development of their spiritual lives. It is my conviction that one of the requirements of church membership should be immediate enrollment and participation in a program of spiritual formation.

Progression is, furthermore, dependent upon *visibility*. The church-wide program of spiritual formation must be kept before the congregation continually, in one way or another. There are innumerable ways to insure such visibility.

The monthly calendar of the church should list all the spiritual formation activities. I like the way it was done at Centenary Church. One side on the monthly calendar contained the regularly scheduled activities and special events. The other side was devoted entirely to what was being done in spiritual formation.

Upon occasion the church library should feature either older classics or newer books that relate to the devotional life and Christian growth. Why not a book table or a book room operated by the church where books relevant to spiritual formation may be purchased? An insert in the church bulletin, at least quarterly, describing some phase of spiritual formation or announcing some book in the field would be most contributory to the program.

The director of spiritual formation should be given adequate visibility to the congregation. In the final analysis, the best definition of a term is a living person. Occasionally the director should assist in the conduct of the worship service, and at times make pertinent announcements about spiritual formation.

After nearly a year the program of spiritual formation was re-presented to the congregation at the morning worship services. The director preached and distributed among the worshipers an evaluation survey:

SPIRITUAL FORMATION SURVEY

Spiritual formation is the intentional and systematic process of the opening of the total personality to the Holy Spirit in order to grow spiritually into the image of Christ.

Name _____ Telephone _____

Address _____

Member of Centenary?   Yes _____ No _____

1. My interest in Spiritual formation is:
   Little _____ Moderate _____ Much _____

2. I am now participating in Spiritual formation:
   Privately (alone) _____
   Describe activities _____

   _____

   Corporately (with others) _____
   Describe activities _____

   _____

3. I wish to begin participating in a guided plan of Spiritual formation under the auspices of Centenary:
   Yes _____ No _____
   I am interested in the following areas: (Give order of preference—1, 2, 3, etc.)

   Bible Study _____   Community _____
   Theological Study _____   Stewardship _____
   Devotional Literature _____   Witnessing/Evangelism _____
   Prayer _____   Service _____
   Spiritual Disciplines _____   Psycho-Social Growth _____

4. I am interested in a short term class in Spiritual formation (4–6 weeks) during the Sunday school hours:
   Yes _____ No _____

There is always opportunity to plan for special features that focus upon spiritual formation. Such events as Bible conferences, prayer conferences, personal awareness seminars, spiritual life missions, etc., are appealing and meaningful. At Centenary we celebrated the one hundreth anniversary of the birth of E. Stanley Jones, apostle of spiritual formation of the twentieth century.

EVALUATION

Likewise, every program of spiritual formation, in order to progress, needs regular times of *evaluation*. It is debatable as to how soon after the inauguration of a program evaluation should begin. This will have to be decided in the light of the situation in the local church. But when the group decides to begin the evaluating process, it must develop adequate measurement instruments. Evaluate the work of the leaders in each of the areas. Consider such questions as these: (1) What are we doing to learn whether we are meeting the needs of those attending our groups? (2) What are we doing to help persons think for themselves, which is so essential in the process of spiritual growth? (3) Are we providing an atmosphere of openness? (4) Is our attitude toward those we are trying to help an authentic expression of our own participation in spiritual formation? (5) What are we doing to foster a spirit of community?

Evaluate the total program regularly. We need to ask: (1) Is the overall program really suited to our congregation? (2) Are we dealing adequately, in the initial stages, with what is basic in each of the areas? (3) Is there a satisfactory sequence in what is being offered in each of the areas? (4) Does our program have the flexibility to permit participants to move naturally from one phase to another? (5) What revisions in the program are needed immediately in order to provide for greater effectiveness? (6) What are we doing to guarantee a long-range continuance of the program?

Of course, the process of evaluation must include a means by which participants may judge their own spiritual growth, or failure to grow, as a result of their participation in the program. In chapter 5 the process of personal evaluation was discussed in some detail.

A final stage in progression may be spoken of as *projection*.

This relates to the future of the program of spiritual formation as it continues to develop in the life of the church. Such plans for projection grow out of the original statement of purpose and also out of the findings of the evaluative process.

Let it suffice to mention at least three issues involved in effective projection. First, how can new participants in the program of spiritual formation be enrolled regularly? It would be an anomaly if at the time the church membership was increasing, spiritual formation activities were but maintaining the status quo. Progress is the normal mood of the Christian church, but it must be manifest in every area of the life of the church.

Second, how can we provide for the transition of those already enrolled in one phase of the program into new and needed areas? For illustration, a person must not be satisfied to participate permanently only in Bible study or prayer areas. Every Christian needs also to get into other areas such as stewardship and evangelism and service. The church-wide program of spiritual formation must provide both the structure and spiritual incentive for such transitional participation.

The Centenary Model faced this issue and adopted the following proposal:

> Each area of spiritual formation should have a class beginning at each quarter, but class length is not limited to a quarter. It is recommended that shorter-term classes be offered whenever practical. If a given class exceeds a quarter, the sponsoring spiritual formation area is to offer another class beginning at the quarter.

> Each area is to provide information concerning the next quarter's classes to the administrative secretary four weeks prior to the end of the quarter. Class leaders will present synopses of the next quarter's classes to their class two weeks prior to the end of the quarter.

A third concern in the projection phase relates to new areas in spiritual formation that need to be explored. How do we identify them? How do we plan for such areas to be offered to the congregation? How do we proceed to implement activity in each of them?

So five essential stages in the development of a plan of spiritual formation in the local church have been suggested:

Preparation
Planning
Participation
Procedures
Progression

Many of the comments have been general, although certain specifics already experienced in the Centenary Model have been mentioned. The essential thing for a local church is to discover the functional validity of such a series of stages and make appropriate application to the particular circumstances at hand.

EPILOGUE

This has been a book about spiritual formation, with particular attention to the local church's responsibility for providing a program of spiritual formation for its members.

The evidence is accumulating. No longer can the local church afford to take lightly this matter of personal spiritual growth. In recent years it has seemed that primary attention in the church has often been focused upon social issues rather than upon personal concerns. Too often the church has thought and planned almost exclusively in terms of the world rather than the individual. There is still a tendency to label those persons who are concerned about spiritual growth as "over-pious," "other-worldly," "not with it."

But the church must return to its spiritual responsibility for persons. A renewed interest in the Bible has led to the rediscovery of this truth. Take the church nearest Jesus—the early church—if we had only the record in the book of Acts we would be led to believe that evangelism is the sole responsibility of the church. But we have also the New Testament epistles, and these are concerned intensely with the spiritual growth of those who have been evangelized. Early in this volume we looked at the biblical emphasis upon spiritual formation.

The testimony of church history cries out for a contemporary emphasis upon spiritual formation. It can be documented that every significant revival period in Christian history has been accompanied by focused attention upon personal spiritual experience and by a serious concern for personal growth in the Christian life.

It is significant to recall that the spirituality of the church during medieval Christianity—the so-called dark ages—was maintained largely by individuals. Many of these withdrew from participation in the highly institutionalized structure of the church into monasteries and communal groups, and there sought to preserve the treasures of the Christian faith. Others established disciplined orders which went out into society to minister to the spiritual needs of persons, needs that were ignored by an authoritarian ecclesiasticism.

The saints of the ages insist upon the necessity of spiritual formation. Every century of Christian history has produced its greathearts of the faith who have demonstrated personally and exhorted others concerning the priorities of growth in personal spiritual experience and life. All the devotional classics are manuals of spiritual growth. In these, every writer bears witness to the indispensability of spiritual growth and goes to great lengths to describe for others the means and avenues of such growth.

Those who longed to grow spiritually found themselves helped immeasurably by others who were also growing. For illustration, Abbé Huvelin, as a spiritual director, profoundly influenced Baron Friedrich von Hugel; and he in turn directed and helped Evelyn Underhill, contemporary leader in the spiritual life. Who would presume to try to enumerate all whom Evelyn Underhill has helped through her writings and ministries?

Father Daignault, of the Society of Jesus, was the spiritual director of Janet Erskine Stuart (1857–1914), who became the superior general of the Society of the Sacred Heart. Spiritual writings contain innumerable letters telling of Mother Stuart's influence on others. She was spoken of as "the very channel of God's grace to souls." One wrote of her, "Her words and prayers changed me at once."

Contemporary greathearts of the faith are just as vocal in their concern for personal spiritual growth. I think of the extensive writings of E. Stanley Jones. All of his devotional books are replete with helps and practical procedures for balanced Christian growth.

Even the titles of Dr. Jones's books enforce the imperative of spiritual growth. *Growing Spiritually* is the norm for the Christian. *The Way* for the Christian is the way of prayer, of discipline, of simplicity, of love, of power. The secret of spiritual formation is being *In Christ*. The believer is always to be concerned about *Christian Maturity*, especially maturing in love. *Abundant Living* is the inevitable result of spiritual growth.

I think also of W. E. Sangster, England's gift to world Methodism in this century, and undoubtedly one of the spiritual giants of our day. All of his preaching and writing was colored by his concern that Christians grow and mature. In one of his well-known books, *The Secret of Radiant Life*, he deals exclusively with what he has discovered as the ingredients in spiritual formation and the secrets of masterful spiritual living.

I heard Dr. Sangster preach many times. Often I find myself remembering something he said in his sermons. I shall never forget his sermon on the text "But He giveth more grace." This was a sermon that not only spotlighted the imperative of personal spiritual growth, but also illumined the means of such growth—to appropriate the grace of God as it is given and to keep on appropriating it because He is always giving *more* grace in response to the use of the grace already given.

I want Frank Laubach to join my triumvirate of contemporary spiritual greathearts. My wife and I have most of his published writings. But as I have already mentioned, we also have in our cherished possession approximately 125 typed pages of his devotional notes. Some, but not all, of this material has been published.

In our pursuit of spiritual formation we took the first 125 days of our formal retirement to study what Dr. Laubach has written. The contents are almost entirely personal. You may have imagined this after reading the many quotes from Laubach in this book. He was deeply and passionately concerned about his own spiritual growth which at times he considered painfully slow and ashamedly inadequate. But he also wrote for others, and his message about the imperative of spiritual growth is unmistakably clear. I would summarize it all in his own words: "You can do no more than you are."

Contemporary theological education is also being awakened to its responsibility for spiritual formation. The inaugural issue of *The Princeton Seminary Bulletin* contains the messages and lectures delivered on the occasion of the inauguration of the new president of Princeton Theological Seminary.

One of the messages, entitled "For the Work of Ministry," was delivered by J. Randolph Taylor, immediate past moderator of the reunited Presbyterian Church (U.S.A.). The closing section of his message dealt with maturity as one of the responsibilities of ministry. Dr. Taylor is clear and convincing in his statement concerning the responsibility of a theological seminary to participate in the process of maturity in the lives of Christians. Here are his own words:

> . . . so what is the seminary? A seminary literally is a seedbed, a growing place that helps growing people to go out to help people grow. . . .
>
> How do we help people to grow to maturity? That's the discipline of this community, as we grow into him who is the Head. We are cursed in the church with too low an ideal. We are cursed in the church with too comfortable a standard. . . . The apostle's [Paul's] insight is that . . . we are called into the future for ministry and for unity and for maturity."[1]

But perhaps the most convincing evidence of the need for spiritual formation is to be found in your own local church. Take a careful, honest, and concerned look at your church. Do not minimize all its strong points—growing membership, capable staff, adequate facilities, attractive programs, balanced budget, social contacts, and the like.

But in spite of these plus factors is your local church all that it ought to be? What percentage of those whose names are on the church roll attend worship services regularly? How active are members in church affairs? Is it a problem to find officials and teachers who are willing to serve? How extensive is the stewardship response on the part of members? Is there an evangelistic and missionary passion? Are members really concerned about people outside the membership of the church?

In my travels and ministries, I frequently hear such statements as these from ministers: "I can't get my people to do anything about the church except on Sunday morning"; "I had to give up Sunday evening and mid-week services"; "The people seem to put everything else first, especially during football or basketball season"; "The people react adversely when I get either too evangelistic or too ethical in my preaching"; "Most of the folks are afraid of a healing ministry in the church."

Doesn't the local church really need something? Actually, it needs to be awakened—to become alive—to become aware—to become concerned. It needs to raise its spiritual standards and to have its sense of spiritual values quickened.

The closing years of the twentieth century are no different from any other age. The agonizing cry for spiritual renewal in the church is heard in many quarters. And it will be answered only in the same way, as in other ages; that is, by a fresh manifestation of the Holy Spirit within professing Christians who are becoming living illustrations of growth and maturity in the Christian faith. Members of the body of Christ must become participants in a Spirit-planned, Spirit-guided, Spirit-energized program of spiritual formation.

Such a conviction is supported by the positive testimonies of church members who have either participated in or who are participating in a church-wide program of spiritual formation. We hear them say, "This enabled me to find myself"; "I understand now what it means to know God personally"; "During my activity in spiritual formation I rediscovered what I believe about Jesus Christ"; "I know now how to replenish my inner spiritual reserves"; "I never would have made it during recent stressful experiences without the contributions of spiritual formation to my life."

On an evaluative survey sheet one of the members at Centenary Church wrote, "Thanks for starting this project. God has instigated some miraculous happenings in my life as a result."

The evidence is in. The need for spiritual formation in the local church is clearly identifiable. The possibility of spiritual formation is a gift of God's grace. Limitless opportunities are before the local church to provide spiritual formation for its members.

What are you going to do about it—you, the dedicated layperson, pastor, minister of Christian education, minister of evangelism, minister of youth, Sunday school teacher, concerned church official?

Andre Maurois told this story about the distinguished French Marshal Lyautey. Inspecting war devastation in North Africa, he found a cedar grove shelled to matchsticks. "We must replant it," he said to an aide.

"But," said the aide, "it takes 2000 years to grow cedars like these."

"Then," answered the marshal, "we must get busy at once."

NOTE

[1]J. Randolph Taylor, "For the Work of Ministry," *The Princeton Seminary Bulletin* (new series) 5, no. 2 (1984): 105.

APPENDIX A

BIBLE STUDY

A study of the Bible is essential to spiritual formation. Jesus reminds us, "My words are spirit and they are life" (John 6:63). The apostle Paul exhorts us to "study to show ourselves approved unto God . . . rightly dividing the word of truth" (2 Tim. 2:15).

Martin Luther warned against merely studying writings about the Bible rather than the Holy Scriptures themselves. Our spiritual father, John Wesley, wrote in the preface to his Standard Sermons:

> To candid, reasonable men, I am not afraid to lay open what have been the inmost thoughts of my heart . . . I want to know one thing—the way to heaven: how to land safe on that happy shore. God Himself has condescended to teach the way; for this very end He came from heaven. He hath written it down in a book. O give me that book! At any price, give me the book of God! I have it; here is knowledge enough for me.

Two of our contemporaries are just as insistent upon the imperative of Bible study in spiritual formation. A. W. Tozer writes, "Of all the means God uses (to bring many sons unto glory), the Bible is the best. The Word of God well understood and religiously obeyed is the shortest route to spiritual perfection."

Frank Laubach shares with us his deep convictions about Bible study when he says, "To be Christlike means to study the life of Christ until we know Him intimately in all His words and all His deeds. This means study of the Bible, especially of the Gospels."

Initially, the following opportunities for Bible study as an aid to spiritual growth are being offered:

1. Introductory Bible Study—basic principles of Christian faith and living
2. Survey of the Bible—a short-term look at the Bible as a whole

3. Bible Study That Works—a "how to" course on studying the Bible
4. Study of an individual book of the Bible (to be selected)
5. Bible Alive Series—Gospel According to Matthew
6. Topical Bible Study—the first area will be Christian marriage.

The Bible study area in the spiritual formation program will be coordinated with the work of the Education Work Area.

DISCUSSION QUESTIONS

Bible Study

1. What is the significance of the Bible for the individual Christian and for the church?
2. How are the authority of the Bible and its inspiration related?
3. How do we discover the meaning of Scripture passages?
4. How do we apply biblical teachings to everyday life?

THEOLOGICAL STUDY

Theological study is an essential element in the process of spiritual formation. We need to gain an understanding of the basic doctrines of the Christian faith and the distinctive beliefs of Methodism.

Ofttimes the word "theology" has been grossly misunderstood by laypersons. Really, it's a practical word, for thoughtful Christians are continually asking theological questions, even though they may not identify them as such.

Theology is one's reflection upon God, a study of what He has revealed about Himself, and an attempt to gain a satisfying understanding of God's relation to His creatures and His creation.

Theology is needed to sustain spiritual experience and activity. Only as we gain insights into God's relationship to and His support of what we profess and do in His name can such spiritual activity be continued. Often Jesus asked His disciples: "What do you think?" The apostle Paul insisted that Christians be able "to give a reason for the hope which was in them."

We also need theological truth in order to be radiant

Christians. I read a most interesting article recently entitled "Burning Hearts Are Not Nourished by Empty Heads." The gist of the article is that Christianity is an intellectual faith; there is a primacy of the intellect in the Christian life as well as a primacy of the heart. In response to the question: "Why bother, then, with religious thought, or speak at all of the primacy of the mind?", the author replies: "Precisely for the sake of the heart; how can we love what we do not understand?"

Just so, we need theological truth to be obedient Christians. Obedience demands knowledge. We cannot be obedient to that of which we are ignorant. The writer of Hebrews says that the laws of God must be written on both the mind and the heart (8:10, TEV).

The theological study area in Centenary's spiritual formation program is offering these opportunities:

1. A class in basic theological studies
2. A class in the theology of Methodism

DISCUSSION QUESTIONS

Theological Study

1. What is theology? Why are laypeople often afraid of the term?
2. Why is theological study as necessary for laity as for clergy?
3. Are there some areas of Christian theology which are of more significance than others to laypersons?
4. What are the salient doctrines in your personal theology of the Christian faith and the Christian life?

DEVOTIONAL LITERATURE

The saints of the centuries have much to tell us about spiritual formation. That is why one of the areas in Centenary's program of Spiritual formation is the study of devotional literature. We need to develop our own personal devotional lives through a study of the writings of the spiritual leaders of the Christian centuries.

A study of great devotional literature reveals the true nature of sainthood. We are enabled to understand what is involved in our contemporary discipleship. As one has written:

Why were the saints, saints? Because they were cheerful when it was difficult to be cheerful, patient when it was difficult to be patient; and because they pushed on when they wanted to stand still, and kept silent when they wanted to talk, and were agreeable when they wanted to be disagreeable.

The saints continually point us to Jesus Christ. After reading one of the Christian classics, Frank Laubach, a contemporary saint, wrote:

God, I thank Thee for those above me who beckon to me to rise to their levels and far above them to Christ still beckoning to us all to rise to His level.

How true it is that in any century we must know the saints, the devotional literature, and the religious practices, if we would really grasp the meaning of Christian thought and living.

Our focus upon devotional literature will begin with a survey of selected devotional writings. We will be using the set of twenty-nine booklets published by The Upper Room under the title "Selections from Great Devotional Classics." Think of the tremendous spiritual insights when we study what such greathearts of the faith as the following have written: St. Francis of Assisi, Francis de Sales, John Bunyan, Martin Luther, Thomas à Kempis, Juliana of Norwich, Henry Scougal, John Woolman, John Wesley, Thomas Coke, Francis Asbury, Jeremy Taylor, John Knox, George Fox, Bernard of Clairvaux, Brother Lawrence, Augustine, Fénelon, William Law, Søren Kierkegaard, Henry Martyn, Evelyn Underhill, and Thomas Kelly.

Later, study groups focusing on a single devotional classic will be formed.

DISCUSSION QUESTIONS

Devotional Literature

1. Why are most contemporary Christians ignorant of the devotional literature of the centuries?
2. Does the church have a responsibility to help re-educate people in the discipline of reading?
3. How can we help persons discover the spiritual treasures in classical devotional literature?

4. How can a plan of personal study of devotional literature be developed? a plan of corporate study?

PRAYER

When a person begins to understand what prayer is and what is accomplished through prayer, one acknowledges that prayer is both essential and basic in spiritual formation. So, in the spirit of a true disciple of Christ, one seeks to learn how to pray and then to actually practice prayer.

Consider the significance of the nature of prayer. Prayer is a dialogue between one's innermost self and almighty God. It is a visit with God, a familiar conversation with Him, a dialogue between two persons who love each other.

Prayer is learning to know God firsthand. It is keeping our friendship with God in constant repair. It is quietly opening a door and slipping into the very presence of the Divine. It is love melted into worship.

Prayer is the time-exposure of the soul of God. It is stretching all of our desires Godward. It is a humble waiting upon God to know His will. Prayer is a sincere request for "marching orders" to serve Christ daily.

Think also of the results of prayer. "More things are wrought by prayer than this world dreams of." Prayer is the mightiest force in the universe. Prayer is the means through which Divine grace is received and Divine power outpoured.

When a person prays, one's thought becomes proportioned and clear: evil memories are purged to save one from distraction; and one can meet responsibility with confidence. The praying person is in tune with life. Prayer means asking God for what we lack. No situation remains the same when we pray about it.

E. Stanley Jones remarked: "I find I am better or worse as I pray more or less . . . I can never be better in life than I am faithful in prayer . . . When prayer lags, life sags . . . If you know how to pray, you know how to live."

Prayer is the heart of spirituality; it is the exact barometer of a Christian's faith and life. Prayer is absolutely indispensable in our process of spiritual formation. The great end of our quest is to have the mind of Christ, to be conformed to His image. One of the chief means by which all this is accomplished is through constant conversation with God.

But prayer reaches out—far beyond the one who prays. It begins by changing that person—but prayer also changes other persons—and prayer changes things!

Centenary's program of spiritual formation has significant offerings in the area of prayer. In addition to classes on the meaning and methods of prayer, there will be a variety of small groups devoting themselves to various expressions of intercessory prayer, and also the creation of prayer teams to visit the sick and shut-ins.

The Prayer Work Area is working closely with those participating in the spiritual formation emphasis on prayer.

DISCUSSION QUESTIONS

Prayer

1. What is prayer? What is the nature of prayer?
2. Is prayer limited to scheduled acts or is it a continuing activity?
3. What are the various levels of prayer?
4. What is the relation of reverence to prayer?
5. What is the relation of gratitude to prayer?
6. How can prayer be made a meaningful experience rather than a mere discipline?
7. What part does honesty play in prayer?
8. What is meant by "focused" praying?

SPIRITUAL DISCIPLINES

At the heart of Christian discipleship is disciplined living. To be like Christ means more than merely to utter orthodox theological terms or to enjoy fleeting ecstatic experiences. Christ-likeness involves commitment to those personal disciplines which our Master practiced and exhorted.

How true are the words of the anonymous writer in *Letters of the Scattered Brotherhood*:

> The way of the mystic . . . is the way of firm self-discipline, of constant vigilance. It is the way of the soldier who needs the full armor of God—"the sword of the Spirit and the spurs of resolution

and action." Or as one has said, "This is no voyage for a little barque, this which my venturesome prow goes cleaving, nor for a pilot who would spare himself."[1]

Centuries before, St. Paul reminded his readers that the practice of disciplines is not only for our present wholeness, but also for our eternal well-being—"to receive an incorruptible crown" (1 Cor. 9:25–27).

So in Centenary's program of spiritual formation, we seek to discover the practice of disciplined living as the divinely appointed means of spiritual growth.

The purpose of spiritual disciplines is to experience the kind of freedom that makes spiritual growth possible. The disciplines in themselves are of no value whatever. They have value only as a means of setting us before God so that He can release into our hearts and lives His grace which is the secret of spiritual formation. In all our disciplines we center on Christ and view the disciplines as a way of drawing us closer to His heart.

Our church's focus upon spiritual disciplines has two offerings to those who have made this area their first preference: (1) a study of Richard J. Foster's book, *Celebration of Discipline,*[2] and (2) a four-month designed experiment in disciplined living. The latter will follow Danny Morris' book, *A Life That Really Matters.*[3]

Foster's book is a general survey of spiritual disciplines. The following disciplines are dealt with: meditation, prayer, fasting, study, simplicity, solitude, submission, service, confession, worship, guidance, and celebration.

Morris' book provides an actual plan for the daily practice of spiritual disciplines.

DISCUSSION QUESTIONS

Spiritual Disciplines

1. What is discipline?
2. What is meant by "spiritual disciplines"?
3. What is the purpose of spiritual disciplines?
4. Where is the basis of authority for personal spiritual disciplines?
5. How can we structure a plan of personal disciplines?

6. Are we dependent upon "the group" to undergird personal disciplines?
7. How do we learn to prioritize our needs in the practice of disciplines?

COMMUNITY

Spiritual formation includes participation in community. Each of us needs to grow spiritually, but we must have one another in order to do so.

The New Testament pictures the church as the community gathered around Jesus. Matthew 18:20 is Jesus' description of such a community: "Where two or three come together in my name, there am I with them." One person is not enough. The Christian Faith involves people in relationships. The development of community is one of the corollaries of spiritual experience.

"Community" consists of two smaller words: "common," which means that people share something in common with one another, such as a heritage or faith; and "unity," which means being one. For Christians, then, community means that we must seek to be one in our Lord Jesus Christ, whom we all have in common, and in our common obedience to Him.

In one sense, community is given to us when we become followers of Jesus Christ. When we are "born of the Spirit," we are actually born into the community of believers. Spiritual community already exists for us to enjoy and participate in and have a deep sense of belonging.

But in another sense, we are responsible for the development of wholesome community. We must do everything in our power to remove all hindrances to community. Extreme individualism, pride, self-centeredness, stubbornness, prejudice, insensitivity and the like, must go.

Just so, we must give ourselves to those things which make for community. Among the imperatives for community are a sincere passion for unity, commitment to biblically supported theological convictions, participation in corporate worship, the practice of confession when required, a willingness to share what others need, and making time for opportunities for edifying fellowship and common ministries.

The secret of community is Christ. As we commune with

Christ we commune with one another. So spiritual formation and community go hand in hand.

In the emphasis on community in our spiritual formation program, we will consider practical ways of building community in Centenary Church; study and participate in corporate spiritual disciplines; and create small groups for sharing and mutual support.

DISCUSSION QUESTIONS

Community

1. What is community?
2. How do we develop a sense of belonging?
3. How do "small groups" contribute to community?
4. How do inevitable "cliques" in organizations hinder or help community?
5. Can we have community apart from the practice of corporate discipline? If no, what are some of these corporated disciplines that must be practiced?
6. How far does community extend?
7. What about the necessity of homogenous groups in church growth?

STEWARDSHIP

Even though stewardship is at the heart of the membership vows of the church, it is a grossly misunderstood word. We promise to be faithful in "prayers, presence, gifts, and service." But too often the "gifts" are what is chiefly remembered, and far too many persons think they have fulfilled all the obligations of Christian stewardship when they make a pledge to the church budget and place an envelope in the church offering plate weekly.

The contemporary church is in dire need, first of all, of discovering the meaning of Christian stewardship and then fulfilling it in all its aspects.

Christian stewardship means three things. First, it is the recognition that all that a person is and is capable of becoming, all that a person has and is capable of having, is a trust committed by God. This means that God is interested in our potentiality as well as our present actuality.

Second, Christian stewardship means the employment of this trust for the glory of God, for the advancement of Christ's kingdom, for the blessing of others, and for the development of one's highest self.

Third, Christian stewardship is the consciousness that an accounting is to be made to one's Master concerning the management of this trust. This personal accounting begins when one becomes a Christian. It continues through all of one's life and will be finally consummated when we stand in the presence of Christ in eternity.

Stewardship relates to the totality of personality and possessions and power. So, the objective of Centenary's emphasis upon stewardship in relation to spiritual formation is to understand and demonstrate the lordship of Jesus Christ over all aspects of one's life.

Stewardship is the primary dynamic of Christian discipleship. Many of Jesus' teachings relate to stewardship. In His climactic story of the Last Judgment (Matt. 25:31–46), Jesus made the faithful practice of stewardship the chief criterion in eternal destiny.

The emphasis upon stewardship in Centenary's spiritual formation program will begin with a study of the meaning of stewardship. The annual stewardship survey of the members of the church will be continued. Plans also call for the holding of a workshop on Christian Financial Planning. All of the activities are in coordination with the Stewardship Work Area.

DISCUSSION QUESTIONS

Stewardship

1. What is stewardship?
2. What areas of life are included in Christian stewardship?
3. What is the relationship of the practice of stewardship to "salvation by grace" and "eternal rewards"?
4. Is there a casual relationship between the Christian's practice of stewardship and material prosperity?
5. How can a person evaluate whether or not one is a "good" steward?

WITNESSING AND EVANGELISM

Authentic spiritual formation is never ingrown. It always begins with the inner life of a person, but it does not stop there. Spiritual formation concerns itself initially with such personal areas as Bible study, theological study, devotional literature, prayer, spiritual disciplines, and stewardship. But the nurture of the inner life is always in order to have an effective outreach to others. It is true that we must *become* in order to *do*. It is just as true that our becoming ceases when we are not doing. John Wesley reminds us that true holiness is always social.

The spiritually formed person reaches out to other Christians in community, to those outside the Christian church in witnessing and evangelism, and to all persons in loving service.

The Christian church exists for worship, spiritual formation, and evangelism. Jesus Himself was the greatest of all evangelists. He trained the Twelve and sent forth the Seventy to be evangelists. He gave the Great Commission as His closing message to His disciples: "Go into all the created universe and preach the gospel to every creature" (Mark 16:15).

In the eyes of Jesus, the world is always ripe for evangelism. The fields are always white unto harvest. How true of our contemporary age! Statistics estimate conservatively that 2.7 billion people in the world including 155 million people in our country need to be discipled to Jesus Christ. Do we really have any idea how many people in Lexington need the Gospel of Jesus Christ?

The Witnessing and Evangelism phase of our program of spiritual formation will work closely with the Evangelism Work Area. Studies in the meaning and methods of evangelism will be offered. Opportunities for witnessing and evangelism, one on one, and by teams of two, will be afforded.

DISCUSSION QUESTIONS

Witnessing/Evangelism

1. What is Christian witnessing?
2. What is Christian evangelism?
3. What is the relation of witnessing to evangelism?
4. What is the relation of evangelism to world missions?

5. How can I learn to be an effective personal witness?
6. How can I learn to be part of an evangelistic team that witnesses to others?

SERVICE

The purpose of spiritual formation is to equip a person to serve others. Such ministry to God's creatures is an inseparable part of glorifying God. It was Ignatius of Loyola who said that the purpose of spirituality is to become a contemplative in action. Miriam Murphy, contemporary writer, in her book *Prayer in Action*[4], says that the vital test of an effective prayer life is the ability to serve others in Christ's Name.

Servanthood is a dominant motif in all of Holy Scripture. In the Old Testament the "chosen of God" were to be a "servant people." The Messiah came into the world as a Servant. Jesus humbled Himself and took upon Himself the form of a servant (Phil. 2:7). Many of the teachings of Jesus relate to service in His Name.

Jesus commissioned His Church to be a "servant church." At the heart of the Great Commission is the call to service. The early Christian church was a serving church, as well as being a worshiping and teaching church.

Serving others is the evidence of loving God. This is the meaning of the Great Commandment (Mark 12:28–31) and the teaching of the apostles (1 John 3:10; James 2:17, 18). Service is viewed as the evidence of love, and love is presented as the only adequate dynamic for service.

So, the program of spiritual formation at Centenary includes a solid emphasis upon service. Such a focus is intended to impress Christians with the imperative of manifesting the "servant stance" of Jesus Christ as the evidence of spiritual growth. Actually, the Service Area is Centenary's laboratory in spiritual formation.

The following opportunities for service are presently being offered: (1) serving individuals in need; (2) serving those in nursing homes; (3) ministering at Nathaniel Mission; (4) ministry through community volunteers; (5) sign language ministry. It is hoped that in the near future a Prison Fellowship Ministry will be also offered.

The service emphasis in spiritual formation is being coordinated with the Service Work Area and with all other areas and organizations that sponsor work projects.

DISCUSSION QUESTIONS

Service

1. What is the relation of "being" to "doing"?
2. When are "good works" really "good"?
3. What is the authentic motivation for Christian service?
4. What is the relation of "good works" to one's salvation?
5. How can I participate in Christian service in the most effective way, rather than merely in a "hit-or miss" way?

PSYCHO-SOCIAL GROWTH

When this area of Centenary's spiritual formation program is mentioned the usual question is: what do you mean by psycho-social growth? The answer begins with understanding the purpose of this particular area: to use the insights of psychology and sociology as a means to enhance the spiritual life of individuals, and through them, the family and community.

The process of Spiritual Formation begins with an understanding of our unique, mental, emotional, and spiritual makeup. The New Testament instructs us to love God with all our heart, all our soul, and all our mind (Matt. 22:37–38). In response to such a divine exhortation, the Psycho-Social Growth Area of spiritual formation seeks to aid the individual in understanding both one's unique and total personhood.

This area of spiritual formation will address both healthy and unhealthy aspects of human behavior in order to understand more fully our human nature. It is believed that the insights and information presented in the classes will help create a sense of praise to God the Father, who created us; a higher self-esteem of our personhood; and a better sense of what constitutes our world around us. It is believed that if one better understands and loves oneself, one has a greater opportunity of fulfilling the second great commandment, "You shall love your neighbor as yourself" (Matt. 22:39, RSV).

We believe that God's grace is sufficient to meet the needs of the areas of new growth in an individual's life which are revealed through the various insights of the Psycho-Social Growth Area. Continuing our treasured heritage in John Wesley, who sought every available means to inform the people of new truth, we too wish to explore the insights gathered by the fields of psychology and sociology. Various relevant issues will be presented. These classes are *not* an encounter group, where members share personal or intimate aspects of their lives. Rather, the classroom sessions are designed to allow an individual both the opportunity to respond to or to ask freely questions pertaining to the issues at hand.

Some of the topics that Psycho-Social Growth intends to offer are: Personality, Self-Esteem, Anger-Stress, Moral Development, Sexual Differentiation, Life's Cycles, Aging, Death and Dying, Birth Bonding, Religion, and Racism.

During the summer months, Psycho-Social Growth is centering on Human Personality and Self-esteem. During the fall months the focus will be on Anger and Stress.

DISCUSSION QUESTIONS

Psycho-Social Growth

1. What is psychology?
2. What is sociology?
3. Do the sciences of psychology and sociology have a relevance to our understanding, experience, and practice of the Christian faith?
4. Do I understand myself sufficiently well to participate meaningfully in the process of spiritual formation?
5. How does a person discover any emotional blocks to spiritual growth? How should one proceed to deal with them?

NOTES

[1] Strong, *Letters of the Scattered Brotherhood.*

[2] Richard J. Foster, *Celebration of Discipline* (San Francisco: Harper and Row, 1978).

[3] Danny Morris, *A Life That Really Matters* (Nashville: Tidings, 1965, 1968).

[4] Miriam Murphy, *Prayer in Action: A Growth Experience* (Nashville: Abingdon, 1979).

APPENDIX B

SPIRITUAL FORMATION

Spiritual Formation is:

—the journey of the person toward wholeness.
—growth in grace and in the knowledge of our Lord and Savior Jesus Christ.
—the process by which the image of Christ is formed in us.
—spiritual development and maturity.

Centenary United Methodist Church has adopted the following statement of purpose in reference to spiritual formation.

"The purpose . . . is to provide an atmosphere of Christlike love and acceptance in which we as a church and as individual members are made aware of all the opportunities for and the benefits of growth, and equipped for service to others and the worship of Almighty God."

Centenary United Methodist Church's plan for spiritual formation includes the following ten areas, in which opportunities for study and experience are offered.

Bible Study

—taking advantage of opportunities to study God's Word in order to be guided in wholesome spiritual growth.

Theological Study

—gaining an understanding of the essentials of the Christian faith and the distinctive doctrines of Methodism.

Devotional Literature

—developing one's personal devotional life through a study of the writings of spiritual leaders of the Christian centuries.

Prayer

—learning how to pray and to practice prayer.

Disciplines

—practicing disciplined living as the divinely appointed means of spiritual growth.

Community

—learning that we need one another in the process of spiritual growth and how to build community in the body of Christ.

Stewardship

—understanding and demonstrating the lordship of Jesus Christ over all aspects of one's life.

Witnessing and Evangelism

—enabling the "born again" Christian to experience spiritual growth through personal obedience to Christ's Great Commission.

Service

—manifesting the "servant stance" of Jesus Christ as the evidence of spiritual growth.

Psycho-Social Growth

—using the insights of psychology and sociology as a means to enhance the spiritual life of individuals, and through them the family and the community.

253.53
ST785

81997

LINCOLN CHRISTIAN COLLEGE AND SEMINARY